**Newnes
PC Memory
Pocket Book**

Newnes
PC Memory
Pocket Book

Ian Sinclair

NEWNES

Newnes
An imprint of Butterworth-Heinemann Ltd
Linacre House, Jordan Hill, Oxford OX2 8DP

 PART OF REED INTERNATIONAL BOOKS

OXFORD LONDON BOSTON
MUNICH NEW DELHI SINGAPORE SYDNEY
TOKYO TORONTO WELLINGTON

First published 1992
Reprinted 1993

© Ian Sinclair 1992

British Library Cataloguing in Publication Data
A catalogue record for this book is
available from the British Library

ISBN 0 7506 0686 X

Printed in England by Clays Ltd, St Ives plc

Contents

Preface and Acknowledgements

Memory management is a topic that has been oddly neglected in books in the past, mainly because it has become really important only now that machines come with 1 Mb as (minimum) standard, and programs, particularly Windows, themselves require so much more memory. To make the subject more obscure, different sources of memory management software use different terms to discuss the various memory regions of the PC machines. This book explains all the terms relating to memory and its use, and the ways in which different software providers interpret the names.

Another important factor has been the rise in the number of 80386 and 80486 machines being sold, making the older type of XT machine virtually obsolete, in the sense that some modern programs will not run on such machines. There are many programs that will run in the normal 640 Kb of memory, some that require *expanded* memory, a few that need *extended* memory, and some that can use almost any additional memory type. There are problems of conflicts of memory, particularly when parts of the MS DOS system are placed into memory outside the normal 640 Kb space, or when networks are used, and some machines also put the ROM contents into RAM, creating another potential problem of clashes.

It is now clear that Windows 3.1 onwards cannot be effectively run on a 386 machine unless at least 2 Mb of memory is fitted, and Windows will not use its 386 enhanced mode even on a 386 machine unless this much memory is available. Rather more memory is needed when several pre-Windows programs have to be run in separate windows, and for really effective use of Windows it is undoubtedly true that large memory resources are essential. At the same time, it is salutary to remember that the majority of PC machines still in use at the present time are 8088/8086 and 80286 types, though these are now regarded as obsolete or obsolescent. It is also important to remember that computer users have been running fast and efficient programs for many years using machines of 512 Kb or less RAM.

Since memory is a topic that is widely and not surprisingly regarded as a mystery by PC users, this book explains what PC computer memory consists of and how it is used. These explanations are aimed at the user with little or no knowledge of hardware, so that later topics on the use of different memory regions can be thoroughly covered. If you have problems with machine memory, or you want to understand the use of memory before buying a more advanced machine, or you want to make more effective use of the machine you already have, this is the book for you.

I have been greatly assisted in the preparation of this book by Microsoft Ltd., Novell Ltd. and Quarterdeck (UK) Ltd., and memory management systems mentioned in this book have been tested on computers from Matmos Ltd. and Micro Surgeons Ltd.

Ian Sinclair
Summer 1992

1 Memory Principles

What is memory?

To start with, a unit of memory for a computer is, as far as we are concerned, just an electrical circuit that acts like a switch. If you walk into a room and switch a light on you never think it is remarkable in any way that the light stays on until you switch it off, and then stays off until you switch it on. You don't go around telling your friends that the light circuit contains a memory – and yet each memory unit of a computer is just a kind of miniature switch that can be turned on or off and which will remain in its setting until altered.

- What makes it a memory in this sense is that it will stay the way it has been turned, on or off, until it is deliberately changed.

- One unit of computer memory like this is called a *bit* – the name is short for *binary digit,* meaning a unit that can be switched to either one of two possible ways.

The memory of a computer consists of a very large number of incredibly small switches, each of which can be either on or off, each storing one bit. There's no other possibility, no half-way position, and therefore much less chance of errors. The turning on and off is done electrically rather than mechanically, so that the action can be fast, but the principle is the same.

The idea of a memory unit being a switch is very useful for explaining how we use memory. Suppose that we wanted to signal with electrical circuits and switches. We could use a circuit like the one in Figure 1.1. When the switch is on, the light is on, and we might take this as meaning YES. When the switch is turned off, the light goes out, and we might take this as meaning NO.

- You could attach any two meanings that you liked to these two conditions (called *states*) of the light, so long as there are only two.

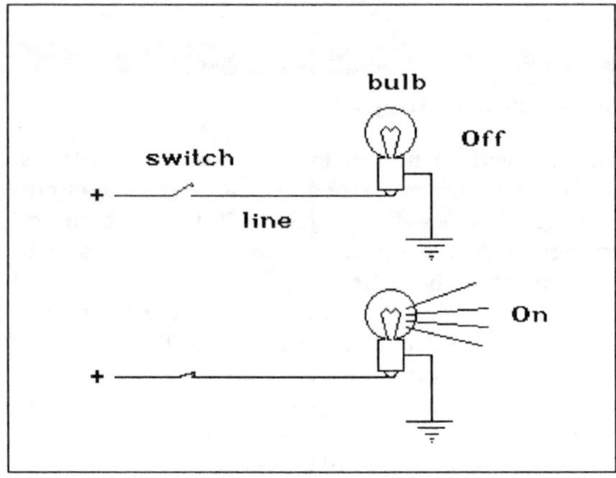

Figure 1.1 A switch circuit that acts like a memory for its two states of OFF and ON.

Things improve if you can use two switches and two lights, as in Figure 1.2. Now four different combinations are possible:

(a) Both off
(b) A on B off
(c) A off, B on
(d) Both on

This set of four possibilities means that we could signal four different meanings.

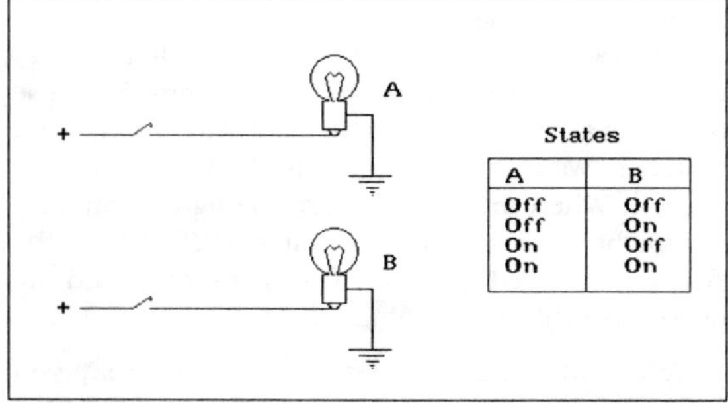

A	B
Off	Off
Off	On
On	Off
On	On

Figure 1.2 A two-switch circuit which can signal four possible states, using two lines.

- Using one line allows two possible codes, using two lines allows four codes. If you feel inclined to work them all out, you'll find that using three lines will allow eight different codes.

- A moment's thought suggests that since 4 is 2x2, and eight is 2x2x2, then four lines might allow 2x2x2x2, which is 16 codes. It's true, and since we usually write 2x2x2x2 as 2^4 (two to the power 4), we can find out how many codes could be transmitted by any number of lines.

- We would expect eight lines, for example, to be able to carry 2^8 codes, which is 256. A set of eight switches, then, could be arranged so as to convey 256 different meanings.

It's up to program writers to decide how to make use of these signals. The set of eight is a particularly important one, because the memory of your PC computer is arranged in groups of eight bits, even though these bits are normally used in sets of sixteen or thirty-two rather than eight.

Binary codes

One particularly useful way of using these on/off signals is called *binary code*. Binary code is a way of writing numbers using only the two digits, 0 and 1. We can think of 0 as meaning switch off and 1 as meaning switch on, so that 256 different numbers could be signalled, using only eight switches, by thinking of 0 as meaning off and 1 as meaning on.

- This group of eight is called a *byte*, and it's the quantity that we use to specify the memory size of our computers. This is why the numbers 8 and 256 occur so much in computing, and why all the important numbers are powers of two, such as $2^9=512$, $2^{10}=1024$ and $2^{20}= 1048576$.

- The way that the individual bits in a byte are arranged so as to indicate a number follows the same way that we use to indicate a number normally.

When you write a number such as 176, the 6 means six units, the 7 is written to the immediate left of the 6 and means seven tens, and the 1 is written one more place to the left and means one hundred. These positions indicate the importance or significance of a digit, as Figure 1.3 shows. The 6 in 176 is called the *least significant digit*, and the 1 is the *most significant digit*. Change the 6 to 7 or 5, and the change is just one part in 176. Change the 1 to 2 or 0 and the change is one hundred parts in 176 which is much more important.

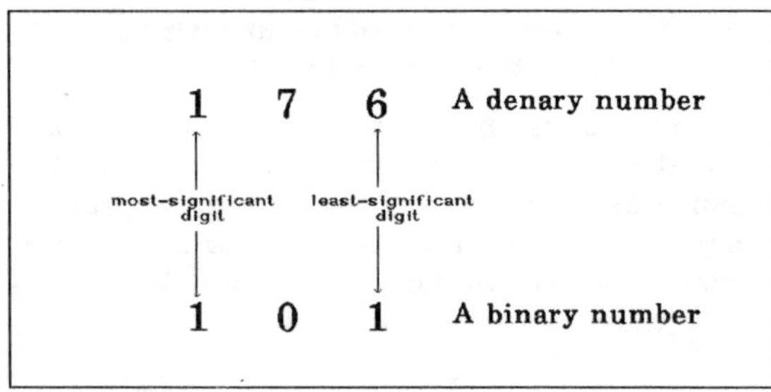

Figure 1.3 The significance of digits, using the position of a digit to indicate its weighting in a number.

- The units Kb and Mb are particularly important. The Kb is 1024 bytes, which is the number that corresponds to ten lines (2^{10}). In electronics, K means 1000, but because binary number are powers of two, 1024 is the nearest to 1000 that we can express in terms of a whole number of lines.

- Similarly, 1 Mb is 1024 Kb, or 1,048,576 bytes. This is the number that we can work with using 20 lines, because it is 2^{20}. Many manufacturers and retailers take 1 Mb of disk capacity as meaning 1000 Kb (particularly for the 1.4 Mb disk which is 1.44 Mb if you take 1000 Kb=1 Mb), but this cannot be done for memory because 20 lines must be used for 1 Mb of memory.

- There is an even larger unit, the Gigabyte (Gb) which is equal to 1024 Mb. Here again, some suppliers take the Gb as one thousand Mb.

ROM and RAM

Having looked at bits and bytes, it's time to go back to the idea of memory as a set of switches. As it happens, we need two distinct types of memory in a computer.

o One type of memory must be permanent, like mechanical switches or fixed connections, because this type has to be used for retaining the number-coded instructions that allow the computer to be started up. This is the type of memory that is called ROM, meaning *Read-Only Memory*.

This implies that you can find out, read, and copy whatever is in this ROM memory, but you cannot delete it or change it. The ROM is a small but very important part of the PC computer, because it contains just enough instructions, 64 Kb at most, to make the computer find the rest of the program (on disk) that it needs to operate correctly: the MS-DOS system program.

o This process of reading the other instructions is called *booting up*, and before this is done the machine is quite useless, able to respond to just the few keys that instructions in the ROM provide for.

The programs that are read in from the MS-DOS system disk or from the system files on a hard disk consist of a set of number-coded instructions – the *operating system* program or DOS – that are stored in a part of memory that can be used over and over again.

o This is a different type of memory that can be written as well as *read*, and if we were logical about it we would refer to it as RWM, meaning read-write memory. It's this read-write memory that is used mainly by MS-DOS programs, and the MS-DOS operating system itself.

Unfortunately, we're not very logical about these names, and we call it RAM (meaning *random access memory).* This was a name that was used in the very early days of computing to distinguish this type of memory from one which operated in a different way. We're stuck with the name of RAM now and probably forever.

- The big difference between RAM and ROM is that each bit of RAM behaves like a switch only while there is an electrical supply to it. When you switch off the supply, the switch action stops, all of the switches are OFF and nothing is retained.

- A memory which loses all of its information when power is switched off is called *volatile.* If the information is not lost when power is switched off, the memory is *non-volatile.* RAM is volatile, ROM is non-volatile.

If you turn on the supply again, the switch action of the RAM will start again – but it will not be set the way it was before. Each bit of RAM may be ON or OFF when power is restored, but this happens at random; the previous arrangement is totally lost.

o When you switch off your computer, then, you lose everything that was stored in the RAM, and when you switch on again all you get is a set of random signals, garbage.

It's like throwing a jigsaw puzzle into the air – you can't really expect it to land still assembled. This is also why most of the programs in MS-DOS that occupy this part of memory are called *transient* – they will always vanish when you switch off, and in addition they will be replaced when you load in a new program.

Back to bytes

Now we can get back to the bytes. We saw earlier that a byte is a group of eight bits which can be arranged in any of 256 different ways, depending on which bits are 1s and which are 0s. The most useful way of arranging bits, however, is one that we call binary code, or to be more precise 8 4 2 1 binary code.

o Binary code, like the familiar everyday scale of ten that we use for counting, uses the position of a digit to indicate its value.

The right-hand digit of a binary number that uses this code can be 0 or 1, and it means just these numbers. The next digit to the left, however, can also be 1 or 0. The 0 means 0, but a 1 in this position means 2. In the next place to the left, a 1 means 4, and so on.

o This corresponds to the normal number system in which a 1 in the units place represents one, but a 1 in the tens place represents ten, and in the next place to the left represents one hundred.

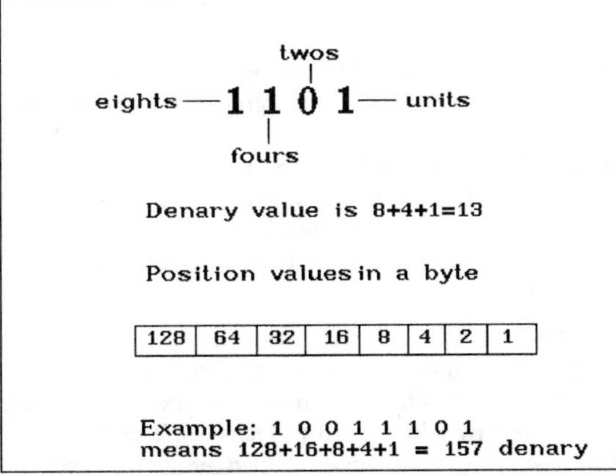

Figure 1.4 The significance of digits in a byte of eight bits.

The whole system is illustrated in Figure 1.4 (above). Each different arrangement of eight bits is used to represent a number which we would write in ordinary form as 0 to 255 (not 1 to 256, because we need a code for zero). Each byte of the 655360 bytes of conventional RAM in the PC computer can store a number which is in this range of 0 to 255.

○ *Conventional*, as used when referring to RAM, will be explained fully later, but for the moment take it as meaning the RAM used for MS-DOS and for programs. It is also called the *base memory*.

Numbers by themselves are not of much use, and we wouldn't find a computer particularly useful if we had to use it to deal only with numbers between 0 and 255, so we make use of these numbers as codes. Each number code can, in fact, be used to mean several different things, depending on the program that creates and uses the codes.

● If you have worked with ASCII codes you will know that each letter of the alphabet and each of the digits 0 to 9, and each punctuation mark, is coded in ASCII as a number between 32 (the space) and 126 (the tilde mark), with 127 not normally used. That selection leaves you with a large number of ASCII code numbers from 128 to 255 which can be used for other purposes such as graphics characters.

● The ASCII code is the one that we use for programming words into binary codes, and anything that consists purely of characters in ASCII codes 32 to 127 is called a *text file*. There are many other codings, however, such as those used for numbers themselves (allowing numbers outside the range of 0 to 255 to be coded) and for other data.

● This is why you cannot read in any simple way the files made by such programs as spreadsheets and databases, and even the files that are created by some word processors. The writers of these programs have decided how they will use binary codes, and their way is not necessarily the way chosen by others.

CPU digression

At this point we need to digress slightly to look at the chip that makes use of the memory, the CPU (Central Processing Unit). Take a look at a diagram of the PC Computer in Figure 1.5. It's quite a simple diagram because I've omitted all of the detail, but it's enough to give you a clue about what's going on inside.

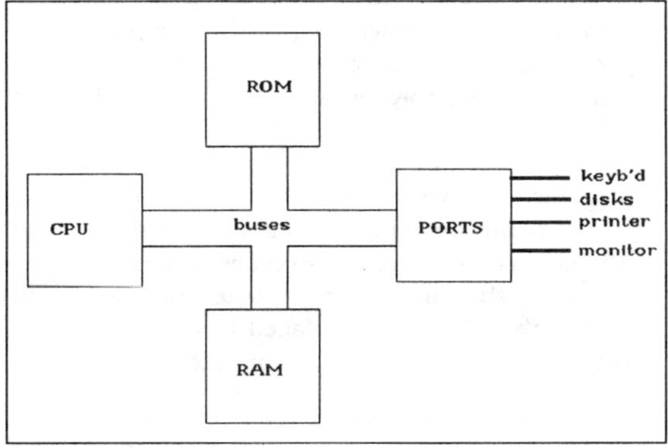

Figure 1.5   A simplified block diagram of a computer, showing the essential parts.

o This is the type of diagram that we call a *block diagram*, because each unit is drawn as a block with no details about what may be inside. Block diagrams are like large-scale maps which show us the main routes between towns but don't show side-roads or town streets. A block diagram is enough to show us the main paths for electrical signals in the computer.

The names of two of the blocks should be familiar already – ROM and RAM – but the other two are not. The block that is marked CPU is a particularly important one. CPU means Central Processing Unit – some block diagrams use the letters MPU (Microprocessor Unit).

● The CPU is the main doing unit in the system, and it is, in fact, one single unit. The CPU is a single plug-in chunk, one of these silicon chips that you read about, encased in a slab of black plastic and provided with 40 or more connecting pins that are arranged in two rows on each side of the chip.

- There are several different types of CPU made by different manufacturers, and the one in your PC Computer will be of a type number that starts with the digits 80; possibly 8088 or 8086, 80286, 80386 or 80486. These are often referred to as the 80X86 family of processors. The CPU does practically everything in the computer, and yet the groups of actions that the CPU can carry out are remarkably few and simple. The CPU can load a byte or a word, meaning that a byte which is stored in the memory can be copied into another store within the CPU, or a pair of bytes (a word) can be copied into a store that will hold 16 bits. The CPU can also store a byte or word, meaning that a copy of a byte that is stored within the CPU can be placed in any address in the memory, and a word can also be stored as

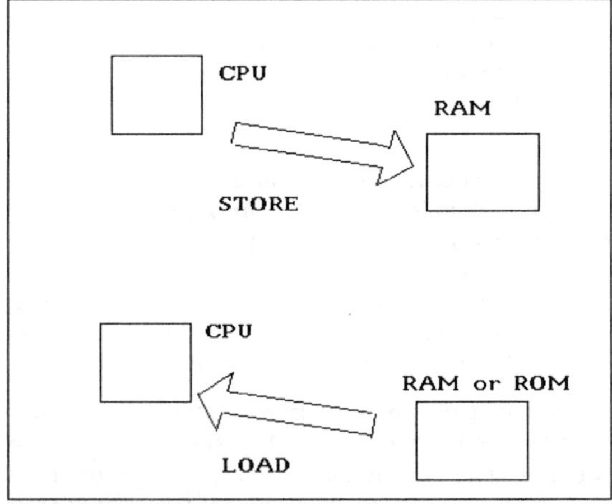

Figure 1.6 The loading and storing actions, which form almost 80% of the work of the microprocessor in a computer. Each is a copying process, so that the source is not changed.

two adjacent bytes. The 80386 and 80486 microprocessors can work with 4-byte or double-word units (of 32 bits) as well as with byte and word units.

● These two actions (see Figure 1.6 above) are the ones that the CPU spends most of its working life in carrying out. By combining them, we can copy a byte or word from any address in RAM or ROM memory to any other address in RAM.

If you don't think that's very useful, remember that the copying action is just what goes on when you press the letter **H** on the keyboard and see the letter 'H' appear on the screen.

● The CPU treats the keyboard as one piece of memory and the screen as another, and copies bytes from one to the other as you type. That's a considerable simplification, but it will do for now just to show how important the action is.

● When you think of it, everything that you do when you are typing an MS-DOS program name is a copying action. You type a letter on the keyboard, and it appears on the screen because of this copying action. It is also stored in the memory of the computer because of another copying action.

After you have typed the program name, it is fetched from the disk by making use of yet another type of copying action. All of these actions make use of loading and storing, and practically all of them are carried out by the CPU (some are carried out by a specialised chip, the DMA chip). Even when you run a program, a large number of the actions are, once again, just copying actions.

o The important point here is that the CPU needs to be able to find bytes in the memory, so that it needs some way of distinguishing one piece of memory from another.

Early memory systems

In the pioneering days of computing, the methods that were used to make memory banks were often weird and wonderful. What they had in common was the use of either electric charge, electric current or magnetism; all properties that can be on or off, or switched to opposite directions.

One scheme used a form of cathode ray tube in which the beam put electrical charges onto tiny metal dots, called islands. The same beam could read these charges off and, because reading always discharged the islands, a complicated method of rewriting after reading had to be worked out. This type of system was the subject of my first years at work and it is fondly remembered only by those who did not need to use it.

○ Many of these early systems were *serial*, meaning that each bit was recorded in sequence, just as information is recorded on tape starting at the beginning and progressing along the tape. A serial system is slow, because if the bit you want is the 229th to be recorded, you have to go through the first 228 bits to get to it.

The first type of memory that was really intensively used was magnetic core memory, and it was in use until comparatively recently on large mainframe computers, though never on microcomputers. Core memory uses a set of tiny magnetic rings, each one storing a single bit. For a typical mainframe computer of the 1960s with 40-bit units and 16 K of memory, this means that 40 x 16 x 1024 rings were needed, a total of 655360 cores.

● Memory like this was very bulky, difficult to manufacture, and difficult to use because reading a core wiped it clean, so that it had to be rewritten immediately after reading.

● The core memory, however, had the great advantage that any core could be selected at random; it was a random access memory.

- In addition, each core retained its magnetism when the computer was switched off, so that the core memory was non-volatile like a ROM.

The alternative to magnetic cores in the early days was a volatile memory that used electronic units called *flip-flops*. A flip-flop could be made using valves (remember them?) or, later, using transistors, and each unit consisted of a couple of valves or transistors arranged so that if one were passing current it prevented the other from passing current.

- The connections between the two parts of a flip-flop ensure that there could never be a half-way stage; if one were on, the other would be firmly off, and the change from one state to the other would be very fast.

Flip-flops were used as fast volatile memory, and when it became possible to make flip-flop units in large numbers on a single chip of silicon, memory units could be made at a fraction of the cost of the older type of memory.

The snag was that these units consumed a lot of power. In each flip-flop, one part is passing current and the other is not, so that current is being passed whether the flip-flop is storing a 0 or a 1. Large memory systems needed a lot of cooling and a large power supply, making computers in turn large and power consuming.

- This flip-flop type of memory, however, is still around, and is called static RAM. Its advantage is its high speed, faster than any other type we can manufacture in large numbers, and since it can now be made in forms that use much less power, it finds some uses even in today's small computers.

Modern memory

Modern memory systems use both volatile and non-volatile memory, but the main memory of a PC machine is all volatile, hence the need for hard disks and for backing up all data thoroughly.

Before we look at the memory chips that are used nowadays we have to see how each byte can be picked out for use, the basis of random access. This uses a system called *addressing*.

o Addressing is remarkably simple. It relies on using a unique number, the address number for each byte or set of bits in the computer.

In an early small computer that used a 16 Kb memory, for example, the memory would have been arranged so that 16,384 bytes could be addressed. This number corresponds to 2^14, so that, using binary signals, 14 lines could convey the signals.

● In other words, if a memory chip contained all 16,384 bytes, 14 connections could be used to select any one byte individually. A further 8 lines could then be used to transfer the signals to and from the memory, so that a chip with 22 pins used in these ways could act as a 16 Kb memory.

● We speak of reading and writing memory, and these are well chosen names. Reading a memory does not alter it any more than reading a book alters the book or playing a tape erases the tape, so that when a memory is read it simply allows its signals, 0s and 1s, to be shared by other units in the computer. Writing memory will alter what is stored in the memory, so that every address that is written is altered.

Memory is seldom arranged in the way described above, however, because it is easier to manufacture chips that deal with single-bit units, or, at the most, with four-bit units.

● For example a 16 Kb memory could be made using 8 chips, each of which gave access inside the chip to 16,384 single bits of memory. Alternatively, we could use two chips, each of which gave access to 16,384 4-bit sets, a total of 65,536 individual memory bits on each chip.

- This type of scheme is still used, so that 1 Mb of memory can use eight chips, each of which can store 1,048,576 bits. A set of eight such chips will provide 1 Mb of memory – see later for why nine chips are often used.

- An alternative, used for large memories, is the 1 M x 4 chip, with four-bit units used in place of single bits. Only two such chips are needed to provide a full 1 Mb of memory.

- Note that memory is always organised in byte units of 8 bits each, no matter whether the computer works with 16 or 32 bits at a time.

Using the buses

Bus is the name that is given to a set of shared lines in a computer circuit, and the name is a throwback to the original Latin *omnibus*, meaning *for all*. The three main buses of a computer circuit are the address bus, the data bus, and the control bus, and we are concerned here mainly with the address and data buses.

o A bus consists of a set of lines that are connected to each and every part of the system that the bus serves, so that signals are made available at many chips simultaneously.

Since understanding the bus action is vitally important to understanding the action of any memory system, we'll concentrate on each bus in turn, starting with the address bus.

An *address bus* consists of the lines that connect between the microprocessor address pins and each of the memory chips in the microprocessor system.

o The address pins will pass signals in binary code to the bus lines, and each binary number used in this way will activate a set of chips so as to obtain access to the unique byte whose address number is being used.

In anything but a very simple system, the address bus would connect to other units also, but for the moment we'll ignore these other connections, and also the methods by which binary numbers are placed on the bus lines. A typical older style PC microprocessor such as the 8086 would use 20 address pins. Using the relationship that n pins allow 2^n binary number combinations, the use of 20 address lines permits 1 Mb of memory addresses to be used.

o In general, as noted above, memory chips nowadays are either one-bit or four-bit types, which allow only one bit or four bits respectively of data to be stored per address.

For a typical PC microprocessor, then, the simplest RAM layout would consist of eight 1 M x 1-bit chips, each of which would be connected to all twenty lines of the address bus.

o Each of these chips would then contribute one bit of data, so that each chip is connected to a different line of the data bus.

This scheme is illustrated in Figure 1.7. At each of the 1,048,576 possible address numbers, each chip will give access to one bit, and this access is provided through the lines of the *data bus*. The combination of address bus and data bus provides

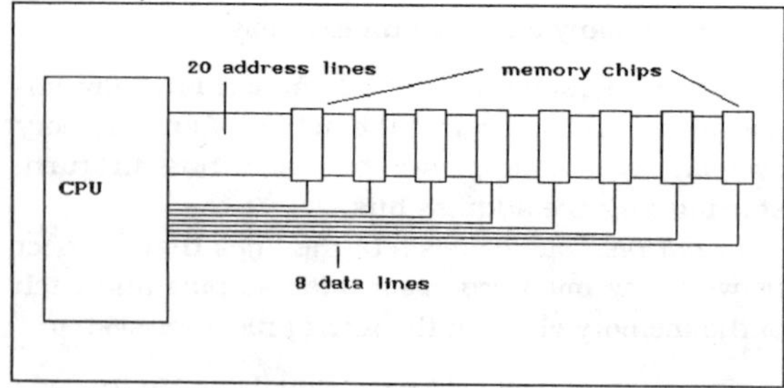

Figure 1.7 The connection system for a RAM memory, made up from eight 1-Megabit chips.

for addressing and the flow of data, but another line is needed to determine the direction of data.

o This extra line is the *read/write line*, one of the lines of the *control bus*.

When the read/write line is at one of its two possible levels, the signal at each memory chip transfers all connections to the inputs of the memory units, so that the memory is written with whatever bit is present on the data line. If the read/write signal changes to the opposite level the internal switching in the memory chips connects to the output of each memory cell rather than to the input, making the stored bit of the cell affect the data line.

● The provision of an address bus, data bus and read/write line will therefore be sufficient to allow the microprocessor to work with 1 Mb of memory in this example.

● For smaller amounts of memory, the only change to this scheme is that some of the address lines of the address bus are not used.

A memory system that consisted purely of 1 Mb of RAM, however, would not be useful, because no program would be present at switch-on to operate the microprocessor.

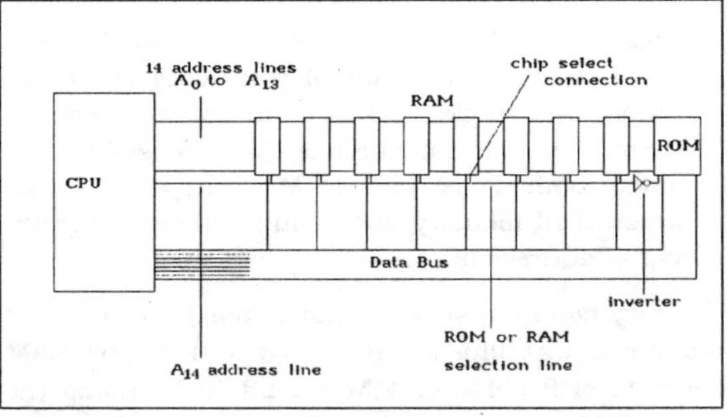

Figure 1.8 Mapping RAM and ROM so that a common set of address lines plus one selection line can be used.

o There must be some ROM present, even if it is a comparatively small quantity, and we now have to look at how these different sets of memory can be addressed. For the sake of illustration, it's easier to look at a smaller system than a modern PC, such as a configuration of 16 K ROM and 16 K RAM.

This could be achieved by mapping the memory as shown in Figure 1.8 above – other combinations are, of course, possible. In the scheme that is illustrated, the ROM uses the first 16 K of addresses, and the RAM uses the next 16 K.

o Now the important thing about this scheme is that 16 K corresponds to 14 lines of an address bus, and the same 14 lines are used for both sets of memory.

The lower 14 address lines, A0 to A13, form a bus connected to both sets of chips, represented here by single blocks. Line A14, however, is connected to *chip enable pins*, which, as the name suggests, enable or disable the chips. The principle is simple. During the first 16 K of addresses, line A14 is at level 0, so that RAM is enabled and the ROM is disabled. For the next 16 K of addresses on lines A0 to A13, A14 is at level 1, so that RAM is disabled and ROM is enabled. The unit labelled as *inverter* ensures that when the A14 line is at level 0 the output of the inverter is 1 and vice versa.

o This allows the same lower 14 address lines to carry out the addressing of both ROM and RAM, using the single A14 line to switch between them. A simple scheme like this is possible only when both ROM and RAM occupy the same amount of memory and require the same number of address lines.

A very common scheme that is used on many PC machines was illustrated in Figure 1.7. The RAM consists of 8 chips of 1 M x 1-bit RAM, using the whole address range (20 address lines). The problem of how to deal with the ROM can then be dealt with in one of two ways.

One is simply to map the ROM over some of the RAM. This means that a range of addresses will select ROM rather than RAM, and the RAM which exists in this range of addresses is never used.

It looks wasteful, but the low prices of RAM chips have, in fact, made a scheme of this type cheaper than a memory built up from smaller amounts of RAM and with no redundant blocks. The RAM or ROM is selected by using electronic switches as before.

Another option is to re-assign addresses, splitting the RAM addresses so that the ROM does not overlap them. This was never necessary for the older XT machines because only 640 Kb of RAM was ever used on these machines; for modern AT machines, using 1 Mb chips, this re-assignment of RAM addresses avoids having unused RAM. Figure 1.9 illustrates the situation, showing memory addresses this time rather than address lines, in which 16 K at the top end of memory is used for ROM in this way.

o The 384 Kb of RAM which is left over out of 1 Mb on an AT machine is therefore usually assigned to addresses starting from 1 Mb.

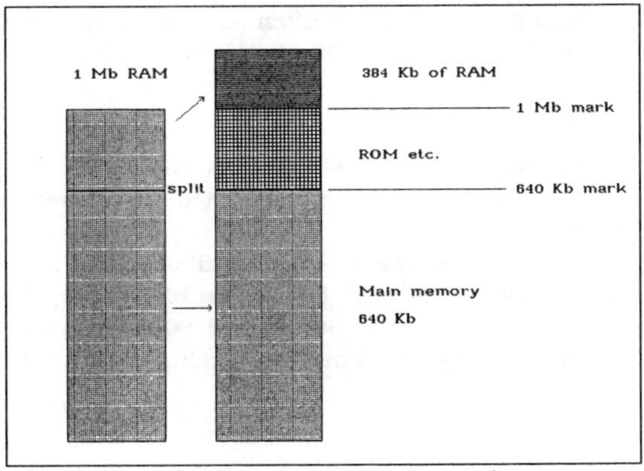

Figure 1.9 Splitting the address range of 1 Mb of RAM so that the upper 384 Kb is mapped to addresses starting at 1 Mb.

The region between the 640 Kb limit and the 1 Mb point is used by ROMs and by video board RAM, and is not usable on 8086 or 8088 machines because they have no more RAM available to use in these addresses – such machines are not organised to use more than 640 Kb of RAM.

o The one exception is the RAM on the video board which can sometimes be used; see Chapter 4.

Since these machines have microprocessors that use only 20 address pins and cannot address memory above the 1 Mb mark, there is no option to place any memory above the 1 Mb mark. On 80286 machines, however, the extra addressing capability exists and this piece of memory forms part of the extended memory which can be addressed, because the 80286 uses 24 address pins.

• Unfortunately, the design of the 80286 prevents this memory from being used in any straightforward way. 80386 and 80486 machines can make use of small amounts of RAM in the address region between 640 Kb and 1 Mb by re-assigning the address range of some of the extended memory.

• This set of addresses is called the *Upper Memory Block* (UMB), and it is often possible to steal the use of some video RAM when it is not needed for high-resolution graphics and use it in the same way.

• The capabilities of chips from the 80286 onwards have not been matched by software capable of using the extra address pins because of the need to maintain compatibility with older machines. This need for compatibility is rapidly vanishing now that 80386 and 80486 machine form the majority of machines being purchased.

Parity bits

When memory systems for small computers first started to expand beyond the 64 Kb level of the early machines (around 1983), designers were very concerned with the reliability of memory. Memory chips at that time had not been particularly troublesome, but the newer designs were of much larger size, and there was a worry that they might fail unpredictably.

○ All PC machines therefore use a *power-on self-test* (POST) system which checks the memory and many other parts of the system. The memory checking is done by using a scheme called *parity*, in which a spare bit is used to act as a check on the others in a byte.

The system relies on counting the number of bits in a stored byte that are set to 1, and setting the ninth *parity bit* accordingly. The parity system can be of two types, even or odd.

● In the even parity system, the number of ON signals (logic 1s) in the byte is counted, and the parity bit is made either 1 or 0 so that the total number of 1s is then even.

● In the odd parity system, the parity bit will be adjusted so as to make the number of 1s an odd number. Figure 1.10 shows what this involves.

```
Parity  Byte
  bit
  1     10011100    1-bit added   (was even)
  0     11011010    0-bit added   (was odd)
  1     11101010    parity error  (was odd)
```

Figure 1.10   Adding a parity bit in an odd-parity system. The first two examples show parity corrected or maintained by the added bit; in the third example the parity is incorrect, indicating a fault in one bit.

- If memory is working correctly, each set of nine bits will always have an even (or odd) set of 1s, according to which scheme is being used.

If the parity is incorrect, it must be because one bit is incorrect. Although there is no way of telling which bit is incorrect, a parity error shows that there must be such an error. This simple scheme will detect a single-bit error in a byte, but cannot detect multiple errors nor can it correct errors.

For many years, PC memory has used 9 bits per byte so as to include a parity bit, and PC owners have always had to pay for rather more memory than users of other machines (though often at a lower cost because memory for a PC is always lower in cost than memory for other machines). Parity errors in memory, however, are incredibly rare, virtually unknown, and the usefulness of parity seems to have gone the way of chain mail armour.

- Many modern chipsets (described in Chapter 6) allow the parity check to be disabled, so that memory can be bought in 8-bit units instead of 9-bit units. Some machines adopt this memory system as standard, so that no parity checking can ever be used unless extra parity memory is installed.

Fixed memory

The use of read/write memory, or RAM, is an essential part of the memory action in all computer circuits, but not the only part. It is equally important to have some memory, though not much, whose content is fixed, unalterable, and therefore called Read-only Memory, or ROM. Random-access will be required to read this ROM, which is why the name is so inappropriate for read-write memory.

- The important feature of ROM is that it is non-volatile, so that the stored bits are unaffected by switching off power to the memory, and are available for use whenever power is restored.

Since a computer cannot be operated without a program (any more than your CD player can produce anything without discs) there must be program bytes available in the ROM memory whenever the machine is switched on.

o The similarity is closer than you might think, because a CD player contains a ROM that attends to the speed control for the disc drive and the positioning of the laser that reads the compact disc.

The simplest type of such a ROM consists of permanent connections to level 0 or level 1 voltage lines. This is done, not by wires but by tiny tracks of silicon in a chip, and the remarkable developments in IC technology now allow economical and comparatively straightforward manufacture of circuits of this type, which have 14 address lines and 16384 connections for each output pin. In other words, this is a 16 K x 8-bit ROM.

o This type of ROM is called a *masked* ROM, referring to the IC manufacturing technique in which etching through masks determines the layout of connections. The making of the incredibly tiny masks forms the main initial cost of production of such a ROM, and the use of masked ROM is feasible only if the content of this memory is thoroughly tested and proven.

A ROM of this type is used in PC machines to contain the important codes that determine access to the facilities of the computer.

o Because the most important facilities concern input and output, this ROM chip is often called the BIOS (Basic Input Output System) chip.

There are other ROMs on board a PC machine, some concerned with the graphics board, one for the hard disk system of XT machines, and others which are placed on add-on boards for various devices.

o Each ROM needs to make use of some memory address numbers, and all of them are located in the range of numbers above the normal MS-DOS memory: between the 640 Kb mark and the 1 Mb (1024 Kb) mark.

An alternative to masked ROM is some form of PROM, the *programmable read-only memory*. This type of memory is not likely to be found in a PC, because it is a temporary expedient, a way of preparing a chip which will work like a ROM but which can be re-used. PROMs are most likely to be found in equipment whose design is not finalised, so you might find them in some experimental add-on boards, but never in the main body of the computer.

Static RAM

Static RAM is based on using a flip-flop as each storage bit element. The state of a flip flop can remain unaltered until it is deliberately changed, or until power is switched off, and this made static RAM the first choice for manufacturers in the early days of IC memory.

o The snag is that power consumption can be large, even with low-power (MOS) devices, because each flip-flop will draw current whether it stores a 0 or a 1.

This has led to static RAM being used only for comparatively small memory sizes. The predominant type of RAM technology for large memory sizes then became the dynamic RAM, since this allowed the construction of very large memory sizes along with very low power consumption and fast access.

o The main use of conventional static RAM is as internal cache memory (see below).

There is another form of static RAM called CMOS RAM, which requires very little power for maintaining its memory contents. In addition, CMOS RAM can be used with a low voltage supply (lower than the 5 V or 12 V used on the rest of the computer), so that it can be kept powered with a small battery when the computer is switched off.

o This is the basis of the CMOS RAM that is used on all 286, 386 and 486 machines to hold values of quantities that you can change but which will remain unchanged if you leave them alone.

Dynamic RAM

The dynamic type of RAM uses a different type of storage system, one that, oddly enough, harks back in some ways to the old cathode ray tube systems. Each storage cell in this type of RAM consists of a miniature capacitor, a unit that stores electrical charge. Level 0 is represented by a discharged capacitor, level 1 by a charged capacitor.

● Since the capacitor element can be very small, it is possible to construct very large RAM memory chips (1 M x 1-bit, 1 M x 4-bit are now quite common), and the power requirements of the capacitor are very small.

● The snag is that a small capacitor will not retain charge for much longer than a thousandth of a second, since the capacitor will inevitably leak.

All dynamic memory chips must therefore be *refreshed*, meaning that each address which contains a logic 1 must be re-charged at intervals of no more than a thousandth of a second (a millisecond). The refreshing action can be carried out within the chip when the microprocessor sends a signal to the chip. The word 'dynamic' refers to the need to have to renew the data at frequent intervals.

o The refreshing is done when the microprocessor is carrying out other actions, so that it is not time taken away at the expense of processing work.

At one time the reliability of dynamic RAM was suspect, and it was this that prompted designers in the early days of the PC to incorporate parity checking into the memory. Reliability of dynamic RAM is now on a par with any other IC components. It is this development in dynamic RAM technology which, more than any other single factor, has been responsible for the simultaneous drop in prices and rise in memory size of small computers over the past few years.

One important point about dynamic RAM chips is that they use a slightly different format of addressing, and they cannot be connected directly to the microprocessor.

- A 64 Kb dynamic RAM chip, for example, ought to use 16 address lines. This, however, would make the chip much larger, and only 8 address lines are used.

- To make this work, there are two additional pins for Column and Row Select respectively. This allows an address number to be sent in two parts, one 8-bit column number and one 8-bit row number: a total of 16 bits in two stages.

- This use of Column and Row also makes it easier to carry out the essential refresh actions, and requires a memory organising chip to be used.

Memory speed

The speed of memory is measured in terms of access time. When a memory address appears on the address bus of a computer system and memory is enabled, there is a short but very important time delay before a set of data bits becomes available on the data bus.

o This time is the access time for the memory, and it is measured nowadays in terms of nano-seconds. One *nanosecond* is one thousandth of a millionth of a second.

A typical, rather slow memory might have an access time of 100 ns. This might seem unbelievably fast in terms of other devices, but it corresponds to a maximum possible rate of accessing memory of only 10 million times per second. More seriously (because memory access commands are never issued one after the other in quick succession) it means that the computer must spend that much time in a memory access, even though it could be working on other things.

- Since many 386 machines operate at a speed of 25 million pulses per second, with each pulse triggering off an action, memory with 100 ns access time can reasonably be considered as slow. Most 386 machines require memory access times of 80 ns or 70 ns, and 60 ns chips are now becoming fairly common.

There are several ways of dealing with a mismatch of computing speed and memory speed. One is the use of *wait states*. When wait states are used, the computer is forced to spend more time on a memory access than on other instructions, waiting until the memory has responded.

- The use of wait states slows down a computer that could otherwise do better, and most modern machines specify zero wait states along with fast memory.

The other ways in which comparatively slow memory can be used more quickly are by bank paging and the use of a cache. *Bank paging* uses memory organised into sets called *pages*, so that one memory access would be to chips in one page set and the next memory access to chips in another set.

- This works because the microprocessor can send out address signals ahead of needing the data, so that by the time the microprocessor reads the memory or writes to the memory, the memory is ready.

By using separate pages, there is no problem of changing address; the next address has already been sent out to affect the other page of memory, and the one that has just been used has time to recover.

o This form of using memory is part of the hardware of the computer. If it is not installed, it cannot easily be added later.

Using a memory cache

A *cache* is a piece of memory, often quite small, but usually very fast in action. It is used as an intermediate reservoir for data.

The use of cache memory hinges on the principle that bytes of program and data are usually read from memory in sequence, and writing to memory is also usually done in sequence. In other words, if you start reading from address 20,000, the next byte will, in all probability, be from address 20,001. There are exceptions (*jumps*) but we need not be too concerned with them at this time.

o If data is copied from the main memory to the cache at a time when the processor is otherwise occupied, reading can be done from the cache when data is required. This reading can be fast, because cache memory can be made faster than any microprocessor requires.

Since it is unusual to have a lot of memory access steps in a row, there is always time for the cache to be re-organised, reading in more data from the memory or, if the cache has been written, writing to the main memory. Even if an entirely different set of data bytes is needed, there is usually enough time between access commands to allow the cache to be filled from the main memory.

o Cache memory can be used within the microprocessor chip, on the computer motherboard, or allocated from the main memory (though usually from extended memory).

To date, only the 80486 chip uses a built in cache of 64 Kb on the chip. This is one of the factors which makes the 80486 chip much faster than the 80386 when both are using the same clock speed. See Chapter 5 for an explanation of clock speed.

Some motherboards incorporate fast static RAM as a cache between the main memory and the microprocessor. Though this is not so effective as a built-in cache, it can speed up the action considerably and it makes the top-of-the-range 386 machines very fast indeed. Once again, this is part of the hardware and if your motherboard does not incorporate cache memory there is no simple way of adding it; you need to buy a different motherboard.

By contrast, cache memory allocated from the main RAM makes use of software, and is a very important way of speeding up disk access (see Chapters 5 and 6). Some disk control cards now incorporate a cache memory which greatly speeds up the average time needed for disk access.

2 Types of Memory

The bottom line

The way that memory is arranged and organised on the PC machine is very confusing and untidy, as compared to the methods used on other computers such as Apple Macintosh, Atari ST, Amiga and Archimedes; the reason for the muddle is also the reason for the success of the PC compatibility from one generation of machine to the next. Programs that were written for the PC in its early days can still be used today, and programs written today are, with a growing number of exceptions, usable on machines of considerable age.

o At the time when the PC was launched, it was fitted with 16 Kb of RAM as standard, with an option of 64 Kb, and it seemed inconceivable to anyone at the time that as much as 640 Kb would ever be needed.

No other desktop machines from that era have survived, and users who were determined to avoid PC use have had to change software with each change of machine. The operating system that was used for business computers in the early days was CP/M, and it worked within a total memory of 64 Kb; it still survives on the Amstrad PCW8256 and 9512 types of machines. Since 1980, machines other than the PC have used one operating system after another, all incompatible.

● This issue of compatibility has made the software rule the hardware, because PC users are reluctant to change to any machine that would not allow them to use the valuable and familiar software they have accumulated. The PC has a larger choice of software than is open to any other machine. The other consequence is that machines with incompatible software have less choice of programs, and the only exception to this general rule is the Apple Macintosh.

● Windows 3.0 and 3.1 have been the first innovations in ten years that have persuaded substantial numbers of PC users towards new software that would not run on older machines, while still retaining enough compatibility to permit older software to be run.

The original design of the PC, at the start of the 80s, allowed for the processor to make use of 1 Mb of memory addresses (Figure 2.1). Of this, up to 640 Kb could be used for read-write memory (RAM) and the remainder could be used for various purposes, mainly by ROM (read-only memory) and by graphics cards and other add-on devices. The operating system, MS-DOS (originally PC-DOS), was correspondingly designed so as to make use of only 640 Kb of RAM as an absolute maximum.

o This is often referred to as the 640 Kb *barrier* or limit, because no version of MS-DOS makes provision for using memory beyond this limit without the addition of other software (memory managers).

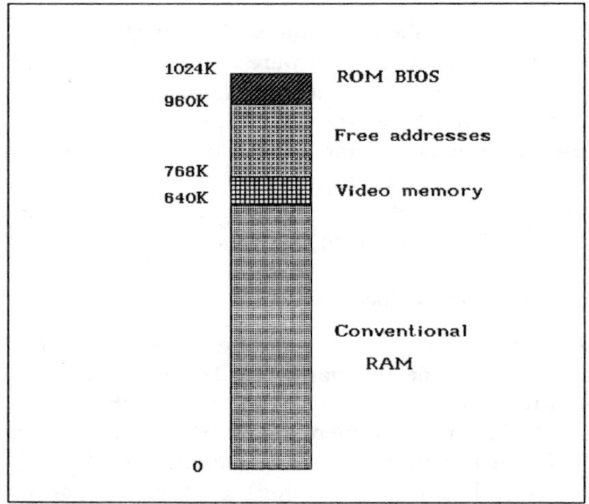

Figure 2.1 The memory map for the original PC/XT machine, which provided for RAM up to the 640 Kb limit. Some of the video memory is ROM, the rest is RAM.

Residents and transients

Programs that you use in your computer are of two types, transients and residents.

- A *transient* program is the more common type; it is loaded in, used, and then replaced.

- Ending the use of a program does not wipe it from the memory. Even if you load in a new program which replaces (or *overlays*) some of the old one, it might not overlay all of the older program or any of its data.

- This is how data can sometimes be retrieved after you have terminated a program, and why fragments of data files sometimes clog up a hard disk.

The other type of program is the memory-resident type, which is often referred to by the acronym TSR,

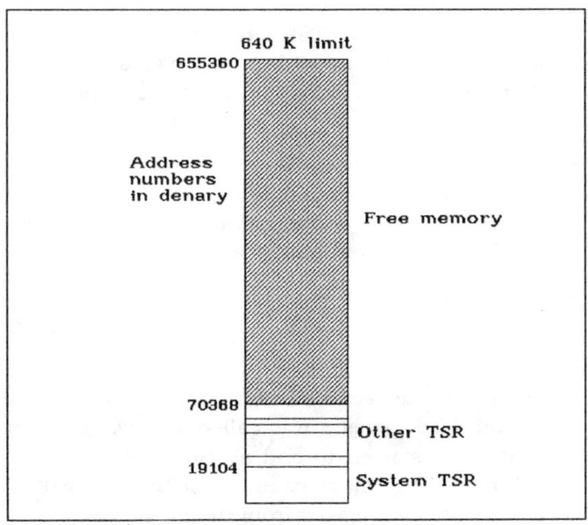

Figure 2.2 TSR programs placed into memory, using the lowest addresses available. Remember that part of the MS-DOS system is a TSR, and essential programs like KEYB and MOUSE must be resident.

meaning *terminate and stay resident*. This type of program is the one that fences off a piece of memory and lurks there, ready for use whenever you need it (Figure 2.2 above). Such a program can remain in memory until the machine is switched off.

o A TSR program loads into memory and stays there, and it also reserves that piece of memory so that no other program can be loaded into that space.

By interfering with the routines that allow keys to be read (*interrupts*), the program ensures that pressing certain key combinations will control the program, allowing it to be brought in and out of use as you wish, even while another (transient) program is running. This is possible because all routines pass on signals by way of bytes in RAM that contain addresses of instructions, acting like junction boxes. A TSR will alter one of these addresses and substitute its own starting address so that the TSR is run each time some other routine is being called.

● This is why some TSR programs can interfere with each other and with programs like Windows that need to use the same key combinations for other purposes.

● Some TSR programs, such as MOUSE.COM, do not require any special key combinations to be pressed to make them operate, they are simply used by other programs as and when required.

● The commands of DOS form part of a program called COMMAND.COM, some of which is resident.

● The key or key combination that is used to start or end a TSR program is called a *hot key*. When a hot key is used to end a TSR program it will still be lying in memory ready for the next call; it is not usually released from the memory.

The important difference between a resident program and a transient program is that a TSR program can be called up while you are using another program, so that the machine appears to be working with two programs at once. This is not so, and only one of the programs can be truly active at any given time, but it does at least spare you the trouble of having to save data and end one program so that you can load and use another.

TSR programs have become very popular, but originally there was no firm set of rules laid down for the way that these programs should be written, with the result that they can interfere with each other and with the actions of Windows.

The penalty for this popularity is, as usual, paid mainly by the XT type of machine in terms of memory loss. Each TSR program takes up memory space, which is memory that cannot be used by anything else. On a machine which has no expanded or extended memory (see later), the space used by TSR programs has to be taken out of the ration of 640 Kb, which is hard enough pressed by the vast size of modern programs.

o As a general rule, you should try to avoid using TSR programs along with Windows. There are obvious exceptions; programs like KEYB, MOUSE, DOSKEY and others are designed to work along with Windows, but others are not and you may find a warning to this effect on some packages.

TSR programs normally load into the lowest set of memory addresses which are available, and when more than one TSR program is loaded, as is normal, they follow one another in the memory. If the programs are suitably written, they should not conflict with each other; several TSR programs provide for changing the key combination (the hot key) which will control them so as to avoid conflicts with other programs using the same combination.

o A more serious conflict can arise when the signals that are intercepted by the TSR programs are not correctly passed back to the system, preventing other programs from making use of them (Figure 2.3).

This is why some sets of TSR programs will work correctly if loaded in one particular order but not if

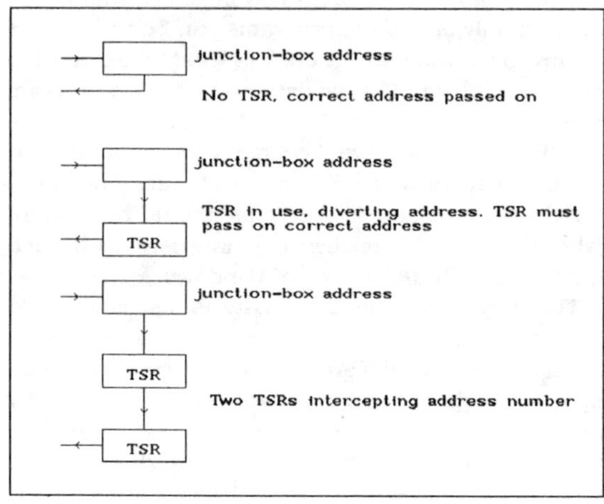

Figure 2.3 A TSR intercepting a signal in the computer system should pass the signal on, even if it is to be intercepted by another TSR.

loaded in any other order – by loading the badly-behaved program last, it does not interfere with the others.

o Problems with such programs can sometimes be resolved simply by loading them in some different order. Conflicts with Windows can similarly sometimes be cured by loading a troublesome TSR program after starting Windows.

Releasing TSR memory use

What is much worse, and seldom realised, is that very few TSR programs provide in any way for the memory that they use to be relinquished so that it can be re-used.

o This can make it very difficult to run some types of programs – notably of the DTP (such as Aldus PageMaker) and CAD (such as AutoCAD) type – along with TSR programs, because there is insufficient conventional memory left over after the TSR programs have been loaded.

If the TSR programs are loaded by commands in the AUTOEXEC.BAT file, one procedure for removing them is as follows:

1 Rename the AUTOEXEC.BAT file as AUTOEXEC.OLD, and make a copy.

2 Remove the lines that invoke the TSR programs from this copy.

3 Name this altered file AUTOEXEC.BAT.

4 Restart the computer, so that the new AUTOEXEC.BAT file will take effect. The TSR programs will not be loaded this time.

5 You can now load in one of the programs that requires maximum memory space.

When you want to resume normal service, you have to reverse this procedure, renaming the stripped-down AUTOEXEC.BAT file as AUTOEXEC.TMP (or something you can remember) and renaming AUTOEXEC.OLD to AUTOEXEC.BAT, then restarting again.

This is all very tedious, and it is surprising that so few writers of TSR programs have made provision for releasing memory. What is equally surprising is that so few utilities for performing this task are available.

o As so often happens, the best utility for this purpose is also the least costly, the MARK and RELEASE set, available as Public Domain software from PDSL (see Appendix B).

The use of MARK and RELEASE solves a number of TSR problems, one of which is the mouse problem, in which the use of some programs that use the mouse partly disables the mouse for ordinary applications (though not for programs that are designed for mouse use).

The MARK...RELEASE system operates by placing the command MARK in the AUTOEXEC.BAT file just ahead of the first TSR program which is to be removed (Figure 2.4).

```
@echo off
PATH C:\;C:\MSDOS;C:\BATS; C:\windows
set dircmd=/w/p/o:gn
set temp=C:\windows\temp
C:\MSDOS\doskey/insert > nul
keyclick
mouse
mark
camera
\hpscreen\hpscreen
dosshell
```

Figure 2.4   The MARK utility put into an AUTOEXEC.BAT file ahead of the first TSR, which might need to be removed. Three TSRs will be removed when RELEASE is used.

- Take care over this; you would not want to remove MOUSE or KEYB or any other TSR program that is essential to the operating system.

- This assumes that the short program MARK.COM is available on the root directory of the hard disk. If it is in some other directory, the full path to the file must be provided. For example, if MARK.COM is in a directory called UTILS, the AUTOEXEC.BAT line would read:

    ```
    C:\UTILS\MARK
    ```

The normal use of MARK...RELEASE provides for removing the protection from all of the TSR programs that follow MARK, so that you might want to re-write your AUTOEXEC.BAT file to ensure that files are in the correct order, with all the TSR filenames that you want to remove following MARK.

Placing MARK in the AUTOEXEC.BAT file has no noticeable effect, other than a reminder on the screen as the machines boots up, until the RELEASE program is run (in the usual way, by typing RELEASE and pressing the Enter key).

- When this happens, all of the TSR programs that have been loaded in later than MARK will be released. This means that the links (the interrupts) that they made with the computer are broken and returned to their original use, and the memory that these programs took up is made available for other programs to use.

- The main restriction here is that when RELEASE is put into a batch file, the memory is not actually released until the batch file has finished running, so that you cannot release memory by putting RELEASE in the batch file that starts one of your memory-hungry programs; it has to be run separately before you start.

Exploring memory

Any program that you use has to take up space in the memory of the computer and you do not know how this space has been allocated. The simplest way is that the operating system (MS-DOS) uses part of the memory, some is occupied by other memory-resident programs, the program that you load in takes the next part of the memory, and the rest of the memory is used for the data that the program generates or loads from disk until you stop using the program. When you stop using a program, the memory that the program and its data occupied becomes available for another program.

o When MS-DOS loads in a program, it reserves all the available memory for the use of that program, so that only one transient program at a time can be run using DOS. The Windows addition to MS-DOS and the later NT operating system both get round this constraint, and MS-DOS has commands which allow memory to be reserved for TSR programs and for running more than one MS-DOS COMMAND.COM file.

In general, the old concept of using one program taking the whole of memory is now out-dated, and many of us are no longer nowadays content to work in this way.

- We like to use pop-up TSR programs, which fence off a piece of memory for themselves so that we can use them at will and keep them in the memory when we stop using them (until the machine is switched off).

● We like to use software such as DESQview or Windows that allows us to have two or more programs appearing to run together.

● We like to use computers in networks that allow machines to share programs, printers and disk drives.

All of these features, which have been tacked on to the original design of the machine and its operating software, make the task of managing the use of the memory more and more complicated.

You may find, for example, that one pop-up program interferes with another one, or that having any pop-up programs at all will prevent you from running a large spreadsheet program or a graphics program. You can find that there are strange after-effects of running a program, such as the mouse not working after a program has been used. These problems arise from the way that some programs alter the memory settings of the computer, and if you don't know what has happened or how to sort it out you will simply have to put up with the problems.

The worst type of problem is when a program that has been running suddenly stops and the screen shows the MS-DOS sign (such as A> or C>), showing that the program has ended. What has happened to the data you were working on?

○ Until the machine is switched off or another program loaded, this data still exists in the memory, but as far as you are concerned it is lost.

Some word processors, however, keep their text data in a form that is quite easy to recover if you know how, by looking for the temporary files. This allows you to save the lost text onto a disk so that it can be loaded back into the word processor later.

Growth of program size

Many programs at the time when the PC was introduced had been adapted from earlier (CP/M) machines which had an upper memory addressing limit of 64 Kb, so that the capability to use 640 Kb seemed very large. What was not foreseen at the time was the extent to which programs would grow because of two reasons:

1 The use of user-friendly screen displays.

2 The use of programming languages that generate much more code than would be needed if the codes were being written directly.

- It seems almost unbelievable now that a good word processor could run in a machine with 64 Kb or less of memory, but in these days it was not thought necessary to keep a mail merge, spelling checker, thesaurus and all the other trimmings along with the word-processing actions.

- Even nowadays, it can be an advantage to use old software because it uses so little memory and runs so much faster. Unless your hand is permanently fastened to a mouse and you find it difficult to type command words of more than two letters, this is the easiest way to use the computer efficiently.

At the time of writing, the XT type of machine is almost extinct (because AT machines can be sold for the same price), and virtually all new machines use a full 1 Mb of memory. If, however, you happen to have a machine which uses only 512 Kb of RAM (or even less), the first step in expansion is to make up the memory to 640 Kb.

- Suppliers of memory components offer kits for upgrading this base memory to the full 640 Kb. Most of these kits are for specific machines, such as the Amstrad PC1512, which were sold with only 512 Kb of memory.

- Chapter 3 deals with the mechanics of adding memory of this and other types to the basic PC machine.

- This assumes that you are going to continue using such a machine. The falling prices of computers in 1991/1992 make the purchase of a 386SX machine very attractive in comparison to the (few) quoted prices of 8088 and 8086 XT machines or even the later AT 80286 machines.

Some machines, such as the Amstrad PC1512, provide for adding the extra 128 Kb on the main board by plugging in memory chips. This requires some practice in handling chips (see Chapater 3). You can also expand to 640 Kb by way of plug-in boards; this is much simpler and can be implemented on any machine that has expansion slots available.

More memory – expanded

It took a little time, but programs gradually expanded in size to fit first the 512 Kb limit that corresponds to eight sets of 64 Kb chips, and then to the ultimate 640 Kb (ten sets of 64 Kb chips) which is the maximum that MS-DOS was ever designed to handle in the first place. The increasing demands that modern programs place on memory, combined with the convenience that additional memory can bring in terms of cache memory, printer buffering or RAMdisk, mean that the use of additional memory, above the 640 Kb limit, is one of the major requirements for add-on cards for PC machines.

- The important thing to realise is that adding more RAM does not ensure that you can use this RAM. Programs that were designed to run under MS-DOS are written to use up to 640 Kb, but no more. The exception is that most programs could make use of addresses above 640 Kb if these addresses were contiguous, meaning that they followed on without a gap.

- Unless you are using a program that specifically states that expanded or extended memory can be used then you will not reap the advantages of extra RAM in terms of larger spreadsheets or more detailed drawings or whatever your application calls for. Some programs can use expanded memory, very few can use extended memory directly (but see later).

- The only *certain* advantages that expanded or extended RAM above the 640 Kb limit can provide, in the absence of extended or expanded memory manager programs, are cache memory, printer buffering and RAMdisk use. These, in fact, require manager programs of their own.

Any additional memory above the 640 Kb limit must use memory manager software because it cannot be used directly by MS-DOS. The memory manager then controls the additional memory in the way that MS-DOS controls the first 640 Kb, ensuring that memory is allocated correctly and preventing conflicts of use.

- This is where complications can arise, because unless you allocate all of the additional memory to some simple task such as cache or RAMdrive, conflicts are almost certain.

- This is because so many programs try to improve their performance by taking short-cuts in the way that they use MS-DOS. Such programs can often also short-cut memory managers, so that the memory they use can be assigned to another program.

- Some software allows for avoiding conflicts. For example, SMARTDrive will use memory as cache, but will yield some of it to Microsoft Windows 3.0 or 3.1 if required, without loss of data. Not all memory cache software will be so considerate.

When you want to install extra RAM above the 640 Kb limit of system memory, some thought and planning has to be used, because there are major differences between the XT and the AT style of machines in this respect. The XT type of machine was never intended to use more than 1 Mb of total memory, which amounts to 640 Kb of free RAM.

o This means that the addressing of a PC/XT machine is limited to an absolute maximum of 1 Mb; there are only 20 memory lines on the microprocessor so that only 2^20, 1024 Kb, of different address numbers can be used for locating bytes in the memory.

Any expansion of the memory of a PC/XT has to operate by switching, so that a different set of memory chips are switched in to use some of the same set of address numbers, making use of some of the address numbers just above the 640 Kb limit. In order to ensure that such switching is fast and efficient, one method that is used is to address only 64 Kb of data at a time (a unit called a *frame*), making use of spare addresses in the range of 768 Kb to 960 Kb. Each 64 Kb frame is used in 16 Kb *pages*.

Different parts of the expanded memory RAM can be made to use the 64 Kb address section (the jargon phrase is that the memory is *mapped* to this set of addresses) as required (Figure 2.5). This, however, is very limiting, and later types of expanded memory boards can address larger pieces – but the maximum gain in terms of running several programs at the same time, using a memory management program, is achieved only if part of the normal 640 Kb of memory is sacrificed.

o In practice, the use of 64 Kb sections, though slow, is satisfactory, and the use of expanded memory is dying out with the passing of the XT type of machine. The cost of installing such memory should be weighed against that of buying a new 386 machine at today's low prices.

The hardware of an expanded memory card is comparatively straightforward, making use of a card which fits into an expansion slot inside the computer. No other connections are needed, but memory expansion by this method also requires software.

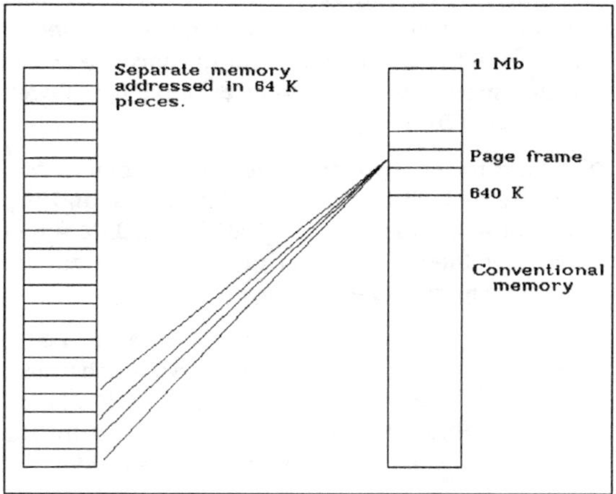

Figure 2.5 Mapping expanded memory to the 64 Kb address range (page frame) in upper memory between the 640 Kb limit and the 1 Mb mark. This memory is usually on a separate board and separately controlled, so is not necessarily subject to the addressing limits of the main microprocessor.

o The problem here is one of standardisation, because unless such software is standardised there is no point in having it.

Making use of this expanded memory requires programs to be re-written to some extent, and no software writer wants to consider having to write 57 varieties of a major program to cater for every possible type of memory expansion board – it is difficult enough having to cater for the major types of graphics boards.

o The first satisfactory agreed standard was known as EMS or LIM 3.2, an acronym of Lotus-Intel-Microsoft, the three corporations who drew up the standard.

This does not mean, however, that all software from these companies will run and make full use of expanded memory on the XT. Expanded memory boards to the LIM standard come with software that allows the use of expanded memory as part of the main memory for suitably-written programs, so that you can, for example, run very large spreadsheets which would overflow a 640 Kb memory. CAD and painting programs are another example of software that benefits from expanded memory.

o A later type of expanded memory system, EEMS, was developed by other manufacturers, and two compromises, known as EEMS 4.0 or LIM 4 (not entirely interchangeable) are now the standard for all expanded memory boards.

If your expansion board is *not* to EEMS or LIM 4 standards, then you will be very much more restricted in what is possible. Usually such a board will come with software that allows the use of the additional memory as a disk cache or as RAMdisk.

• This is still useful, though not so useful as memory that programs can use directly. Setting up a disk cache, for example, can speed up disk access appreciably, a printer buffer can allow you to use the computer while the printer is beavering away, and using a RAMdisk for a word processor spell-checking dictionary can make this action much faster.

• The gains, however, are in speed and not in the ability to use larger programs and more data; nor can you run multiple programs, switching rapidly from one to another.

If you have such a board, you can make use of it along with multi-tasking software such as Desqview to use it for switching in and out of programs, an action which is faster than RAMdisk. If you are thinking of buying a new expanded memory board consider only the EEMS/LIM 4.0 type and do not be tempted by bargain offers of older types. If a bargain board makes no mention of LIM 4.0, you can be sure that it will be of the older, less useful type.

o Once again, though, you have to balance the cost of an expanded memory board and its software against the cost of a more capable computer. If your machine is old and tired, why pour more into it when you could buy a machine of much greater capabilities at today's low prices?

The installation of an Expanded Memory board is mechanically straightforward, amounting to nothing more than inserting the card into a vacant expansion slot. You may, however, need to set switches or jumpers on the card before installation so that the card is set up correctly for the type of machine that is being used – these expanded memory cards can be used on either XT or AT machines. Be cautious about using any cards which require the microprocessor to be removed – this is not a straightforward task for anyone who has not done something similar before.

- Many makes of expansion cards can be bought either *populated* or *unpopulated*. A populated board need only be inserted into the slot, but an unpopulated board (often available at bargain prices) requires you to buy the correct type of memory chips and insert them for yourself. Some cards come with 512 Kb installed and space for further expansion provided as and when desired.

- If the card can use memory in the form of pre-formed strips called SIMM or SIPP, installing memory is very much easier, but plugging in individual chips needs some knowledge and experience (see Chapter 3). You save little, if anything, by buying an unpopulated board unless you have a large stock of suitable memory chips to use up.

Software changes

Once a board of this type has been fitted you will need to alter the CONFIG.SYS file of your computer so as to activate the board, and to copy the necessary software program file from the supplied floppy disk onto a suitable directory (preferably the root directory) of your hard disk.

o The instructions that come with the expanded memory board will have to be rigorously followed, because the alterations to the CONFIG.SYS file will have to specify the memory addresses that must not be used by the expanded memory board.

This has to be done by you, because only you are in a position to know what video card and what other cards are already installed in your computer. Some expanded memory board software includes an installation program which can analyse the memory situation, so making the process much easier.

Using expanded or (see later) extended memory for RAMdisk or cache also requires software to be installed and commands placed in the CONFIG.SYS file.

o CONFIG.SYS is a simple file which is a list of commands, one on each line of the file.

The file (Figure 2.6) consists of plain text, the type of file we call ASCII, which can be created by any text editor, such as the EDITOR of MS-DOS 5.0, Amstrad's RPED, or the Notepad of Windows. Each command line of CONFIG.SYS carries out some

```
DEVICE=C:\MSDOS\SETVER.EXE
files=30
buffers=20
country=044,850,c:\country.sys
DEVICE=C:\MSDOS\HIMEM.SYS
INSTALL=smartdrv.exe A- B- 512 /q
SHELL=C:\MSDOS\COMMAND.COM C:\MSDOS\ /p
DOS=HIGH
stacks = 0,0
device= c:\hhscand.sys /a=280/i=3/d=1
               /h=4:8&:12:16/w=103/t=15
```

Figure 2.6   A typical CONFIG.SYS file, consisting of commands, one per line, that are acted on before the MS-DOS files are loaded. Every command in CONFIG.SYS will result in some memory being requisitioned, and in this example, the last line activates software for a Logitech hand scanner.

piece of configuration, making your computer more suitable for the jobs you want it to carry out.

- CONFIG.SYS commands are carried out very early in the boot-up process, before any other files are read; even before MS-DOS starts up.

- If you change CONFIG.SYS and want to see the effect, you need to reboot the computer; there is no other way of running CONFIG.SYS.

CONFIG.SYS is used to set up a lot of actions, some of which, like FILES and BUFFERS, make use of memory. Because CONFIG.SYS allocates memory for use, its action has to be carried out immediately following a reboot when all of the memory has been cleared. If such allocation of memory took place at any later time, the contents of memory would have to be completely re-arranged.

AT machines and extended memory

The AT type of machine uses the 80286, 80386 or 80486 type of processor which can address very much more memory than the 1 Mb limit of the 8086/8088 chips used in the original PC and XT machines.

- The 80286 machine can address up to 16 Mb, and the 80386 and 80486 up to 4096 Mb. Even the most sprawling of modern programs will fit in these limits. Such machines often come with at least 1 Mb of RAM on the main board (the *motherboard*) and provision for adding more memory, usually 4 Mb or 16 Mb, on the motherboard. This type of memory above the 640 Kb limit is called *extended* memory.

- Unlike expanded memory, extended memory is addressed directly with each byte of memory having its own unique address rather than the expanded memory system of using a 64 Kb set of addresses to use 64 Kb pieces of memory one at a time.

- Programs designed to run under MS-DOS, however, do not make use of these memory address numbers. To do so would make the programs incompatible with the older XT machines, which are physically incapable of generating these address numbers.

- A few programs, notably Lotus 1-2-3 version 3.1, DisplayWrite, and Windows Version 3 programs can make use of these numbers and are therefore incompatible with the older machines. This is why versions 2.2 and 3.0 of Lotus 1-2-3 can both co-exist; V3.0 can be run only on AT machines, but V2.2 can be run on any PC machines.

In an AT machine with 1 Mb of RAM, this first 1 Mb is usually split (but see 'Shadow memory', later), with a lower section using addresses up to 640 Kb, and the remaining 384 Kb located at addresses just above the 1 Mb point (Figure 2.7). Any further extended memory is located in the following

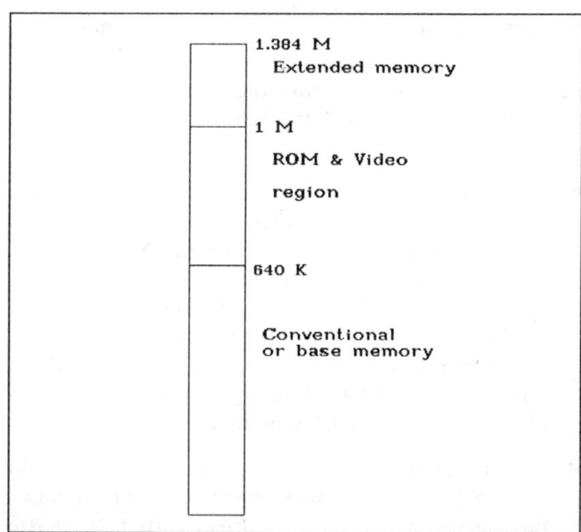

Figure 2.7 The memory map of a conventional AT machine with 1 Mb of RAM, using 384 Kb of extended memory. Using MS-DOS 5.0, 64 Kb of the extended memory can be used conventionally to hold DOS itself.

addresses, joining seamlessly to the 384 Kb from the first megabyte.

- This makes the first megabyte of RAM of an AT machine particularly important. The addresses between the 640 Kb mark and the 1 Mb mark are used in exactly the same way as they are in the old XT machines in order to maintain compatibility.

- Unfortunately, the parts of this memory above the 640 Kb limit cannot be addressed when the machine is using only MS-DOS, which for most of us is all the time.

- Extended memory can be used by programs if the rules laid down by Microsoft are followed, using a memory manager system called XMS. Very few programs, however, make use of extended memory in this way, but two important exceptions are Lotus 1-2-3 V3 and Windows 3.

- Using Windows 3 allows extended memory to be used by any of the programs that are being run under Windows 3. The new operating system, NT, which Microsoft are developing will be able to replace both MS-DOS and Windows in this respect, but will run only on 80386, 80486 and later (yet to be announced) machines.

Where the motherboard of the AT machine does not provide for several Mb of memory, or, more likely, when all of the motherboard sockets have already been filled and you need still more memory, you can install an extended memory board. This is seldom required, because all AT machines provide for at least 4 Mb on the main board, and most for 16 Mb or more.

You can also install an expanded memory board, acting in the same way as on the XT, and this can cause considerable confusion. In addition, the use of expanded memory boards is now being discouraged because these were a temporary solution to a problem (only 20 address lines) that no longer exists. Many memory boards now being sold provide for being organised as either expanded or extended memory.

o If in doubt, always go for the *extended* memory of a 386 or 486 AT machine and *possibly expanded* memory on a 286 machine. The 386 and 486 chips can be controlled by software to use extended memory efficiently, but the 286 cannot. The 286 design does not permit such use by MS-DOS, only by other operating systems which, in practice, have either not materialised or which cannot make use of programs intended to run under MS-DOS.

Extended memory has to be controlled by a memory manager program, just as expanded memory must be. The important differences are:

1 Extended memory is available only on AT machines, not on XT machines, and its use is incompatible with the use of XT machines.

2 Expanded memory can be used on any machine, but was originally intended for the XT type of machines.

3 Extended memory is faster because it does not need to be addressed in 64 Kb chunks, and the extended memory addresses above 1 Mb are contiguous, not split up by other uses.

4 Modern software using Microsoft Windows requires extended memory and cannot use expanded memory in any useful way.

5 Most memory manager programs can make use of extended memory as if it were expanded, to suit the programs that require expanded memory and in addition to allow a small part of extended RAM to be mapped to addresses just above the 640 Kb barrier. Such addresses (the UMB addresses) can be used by short programs.

o You can implement RAMdrive, cache and printer buffer uses on extended memory as easily as in expanded memory, usually by placing an option letter in the command that sets up the software. More commonly now, such software assumes the use of extended memory and requires option letters only if expanded memory is used.

Virtual memory

Virtual memory is not RAM, but another form of data storage system which can be addressed in the same way as RAM. The most common form of virtual memory is a hard disk used in this way, and the aim of virtual memory is to allow a program and its data to be swapped between RAM (in which the program can run) and disk (on which running is not possible when bytes are saved using the normal disk saving and loading commands).

What makes virtual memory different from the ordinary use of a disk is that each byte of a file has associated with it an address number, so that as far as the microprocessor is concerned the byte is stored in a very slow piece of memory.

Virtual memory, like any memory, needs to be managed, and this can be done either from within the microprocessor chip or by other software.

o Using an area of memory as a disk is the opposite of *virtual disk* (using memory like a disk), which is why one well known RAMdrive program is called VDISK.

The more advanced chips, such as the 80386 and 80486, incorporate the ability to use virtual memory, but MS-DOS does not make use of these facilities since they would be incompatible with the earlier machines. Virtual memory is explained further in Chapter 6.

Built-in cache

The 80486 chip incorporates a 64 Kb cache as part of the chip, making the speed of this microprocessor faster than that of the 80386 even when the 80486 is being used at a lower clock speed.

The 80386 chip contains no cache, but the cache memory can be placed on the motherboard. Though this is not so efficient as building the memory into the microprocessor chip, it significantly speeds up the machine.

Networking software

The use of networking provides at least half of all the problems of memory size and program incompatibility. Networking of two or more machines is a very attractive proposition when expensive resources like a laser printer and a large hard drive can be shared.

- Networking allows a program to be run from a disk on another machine, altering files that will also be altered if they are in use on other machines, and allowing the printer to be used as and when it is available, shared among the networked machines.

- All but the simplest networks which use the serial port (but which can be very effective for two or three machines) will require hardware in the form of a networking card. The best known system is Novell, but the immense size and cost of the full Novell network makes this a choice for users of large networks only. Novell Lite is an alternative for smaller scale users, and there are several other systems. For small scale users, the $25 Network from EQ Consultants (see Appendix B) is a very attractive proposition.

- Software is also essential to control the use of the network and to ensure that potential conflicts are resolved.

For example, the software must ensure that when two users want the printer at the same time, one will gain immediate use of the printer, and the text from the other will be stored until the printer is ready. It must also ensure that when one user modifies a data file, all other users of that file will see the updated version, so that there can never be more than one version in use. It must also allocate drive letters for disks that are in another machine.

- Because network management carries out some actions that are also carried out by memory managers, there are many potential conflicts, and it is rare not to experience some difficulties with a network, particularly when Windows is being used (see Chapter 6).

MS-DOS 5.0 is compatible with all networks, but with some precautions. When MS-DOS is installed you run a SETUP program which allows you to state whether or not you are using a network. When you install a network on a machine on which MS-DOS 5.0 is already in use, you will need to use SETUP again.

○ Network software will, with very few exceptions, refuse to operate if you try to start the network from the DOSSHELL. Always start the network running before starting up DOSSHELL.

MS-DOS 5.0 recognises and works with most networks, and problems with the following are known and can be remedied:

    3+Share
    AT&T StarGROUP
    Microsoft LAN Manager 2.0 Enhanced
    Net/One PC
    Novell Networks
    PC-NFS 3.0
    TOPS Network

Some earlier versions of these networks are incompatible, but the most recent versions require only a few setting up modifications that are noted in the MS-DOS README file.

Memory nomenclature

The various different parts of the PC memory have in the past been called different names by different software manufacturers, and this has led to considerable confusion. The following is a list of names used in this book with a note of the other names that are sometimes found.

Conventional memory: The first 640 Kb of memory starting from address zero and used for all conventional programs running under MS-DOS. Also called *system memory*, *base memory*, *low memory*, *low memory area.*

Expanded memory: RAM provided usually on a plug-in board and addressed in units called *frames* of 64 Kb each, subdivided into *pages* of 16 Kb each. Each frame uses some addresses (which MS-DOS recognises) taken from the region between 640 Kb and 1 Mb, and some systems allow up to four such frames to be used, depending on how many address numbers are free. Expanded memory is the only practical system for increasing the RAM of the XT machine; its use on AT machines is optional.

Extended memory: Memory which uses addresses from 1 Mb upwards, and is therefore available only on AT machines whose microprocessors have more than 20 address lines. Extended memory can be used only by programs specially written to use these addresses, such as a memory manager program. It is possible, given a suitable manager, to use extended memory as if it were expanded memory, so that this form of memory is more adaptable. Also called *high memory*, *high memory area*, *high memory blocks.*

Upper Memory: Memory, usually 64 Kb to 128 Kb in size, which is used along with addresses in the range between 640 Kb and 1 Mb. This range of memory, which is also used for expanded memory, can be used by MS-DOS to run programs if a suitable memory manager is running. The memory that is used along with these addresses is usually taken from the 384 Kb of extended RAM in the first megabyte of RAM, making this memory unavailable for other purposes. Referred to also as *UMB* or *high memory* (Figure 2.8).

Remember that the same amount of RAM cannot do two jobs at once. If your computer contains 1 Mb of RAM there will 384 Kb unused by MS-DOS. You can use this for a number of purposes:

1 As shadow RAM to hold copies of ROM

2 As extended memory

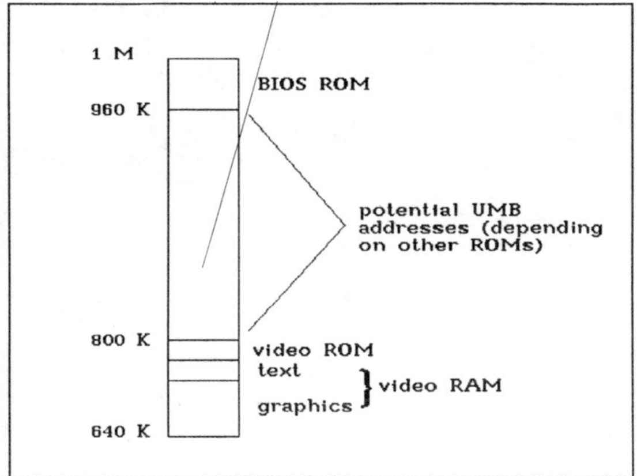

Figure 2.8 The UMB region of memory, where some spare address numbers are almost certain to be found. ROMs in add-on devices may take up some of these addresses.

3 As expanded memory

4 As upper memory

You cannot use all of these at once, and you choose one at the expense of the other. It is possible to use some of this memory as upper memory and some as RAMdrive, or some as extended memory and some as RAMdrive, but the total being used certainly cannot be more than 384 Kb.

3 Fitting Memory

Adding chips

The most elementary and the most physically difficult way of adding memory is to plug the individual integrated circuit (IC) chips into sockets on a motherboard. Later we shall look at methods that use expansion boards or the modules called SIMM or SIPP, but in a surprising number of examples, plugging in chips is the only provision that exists. It is, for example, the only sensible way of bringing up the old Amstrad PC1512 to the full 640 Kb of base memory, and even now there are a few XT machines which make no provision other than the fitting of an expansion card on which some of the memory can be specified as conventional (base) memory. In addition, adding memory to a graphics card or to a memory expansion card can in most cases be done only by plugging in chips.

- Handling individual chips is a fiddly business which requires practice. It is not particularly difficult, but needs some care and attention to detail until you become experienced.

- You may in the past have read accounts of how chips can be damaged by electrostatic voltages, so that operators are obliged to wear copper manacles connected to earthed metal benches while handling chips. Ignore such stories; they apply only to the construction of chips, not to their normal use.

- Modern chips can be handled without excessive precautions providing you are reasonably careful about static electricity.

To start by dispelling a popular illusion, it is quite difficult to damage a chip electrically by handling it. If you are working in a room in very dry conditions, so that you experience a violent shock every time you shuffle your feet on the carpet and then touch the radiator it would be a good idea to carry out your chip handling somewhere else.

o These very dry conditions are unusual in the UK, and even if a room is crackling with static electricity, damage to a chip is likely only if contact is made with just one pin when the others are connected to somewhere else.

There is a layer of safeguards in the form of internal escape routes for excessive voltages inside the chip (protection diodes), so that the chances of damaging chips in this way are negligible compared to the chances of bending the pins when you are trying to fit the chips into their holders.

● Since plastics are the materials most likely to cause trouble with static, avoid using plastic tweezers or tools, trays or working surfaces.

● A wood surface is ideal, because its moisture content makes it a conductor and most unlikely ever to be electrically charged. Metal tools that are held in your hand are also safe to use if you are also holding the chip that you are working on.

The first and most important step is to be certain *where* the chips need to be added, and *what type* of chips are to be used. Motherboards for PC clones are of a fairly standardised form nowadays, but if your machine is one of the 'big names', including Amstrad, the layout is likely to be quite different from the IBM standard.

● In particular, it is likely that a switch, usually of the miniature type called a DIL (*dual in line*) switch (sometimes referred to as a *DIP switch*), or a *jumper* (Figure 3.1) will have to be set differently if you are upgrading a motherboard from 512 Kb to 640 Kb. Never contemplate adding memory chips until you know *exactly* what is required and where jumpers or switches are located.

● If you are adding chips to an expansion board or to a graphics board, the positions for the chips are likely to be marked out clearly. Graphics boards do not necessarily use the same expansion chips as memory expansion boards.

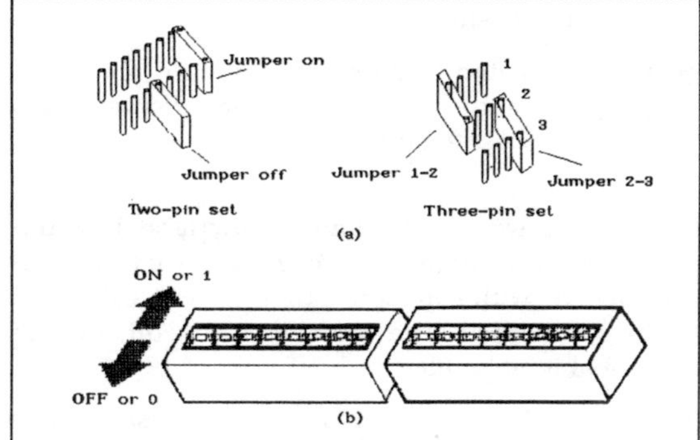

Figure 3.1 The jumper (a) or a DIL switch block (b) will be the normal method of adjusting connections on the motherboard to accommodate signals for extra memory.

The variety of chips is very large, and you must be certain that you are using the correct chips. The important features are:

1 The type of chip: a 41256 is not the same as a 44256, for example.

2 The speed of chip: if your other memory chips are rated at 80 ns, it would be foolish to add 100 ns chips for your extra memory.

3 The physical form of the chip: most will use 16 to 22 pins in two rows. The chips you use must fit the carriers that already exist on the board.

Planning and chip handling

1 If you have a hard disk installed, park the disk heads before starting on the expansion of memory.

2 Switch off the computer and remove mains plugs. Leave the machine for five minutes to ensure that all electrical voltages in the machine are discharged. Disconnect and remove the

monitor if it sits (as it usually does) on top of the computer casing.

3   You might find it more convenient to remove all plugs from the rear of the computer and any that use sockets on the sides.

• If you have never handled anything like this before you should try to ensure that there is someone with experience that you can call on for help if needed. The work isn't difficult, but it's probably unfamiliar.

• For the Amstrad PC1512, all expansion cards must be removed before the memory can be expanded. On straightforward clone machines the cards can normally be left in place unless you find it difficult to work with them in.

• If you are fitting additional memory into a memory expansion board or into a video graphics board the board has to be out of the computer, and should be laid on clean paper or on one of the antistatic bags that are used for packing such boards.

The memory expansion of a PC/XT type of machine to 640 Kb, when there are spaces on the motherboard, is relatively simple if you have ever plugged integrated circuit chips into a board before, and you will normally have good enough access if you simply flip open the lid of the case.

o   For the Amstrad PC1512 you need to remove the top cover and the floppy disk drive (if fitted) that covers the memory chip sockets. In addition, you will either have to remove the batteries from their holder in the top of the disk unit casing, or prop the top of the casing up so that the connecting wires are not strained. If you remove the batteries you will have to restore the time and date settings, along with the items that are set by the Amstrad NVR program, after you have completed the upgrade.

Whatever type of machine is being used, the full set of sockets for the memory chips should now be

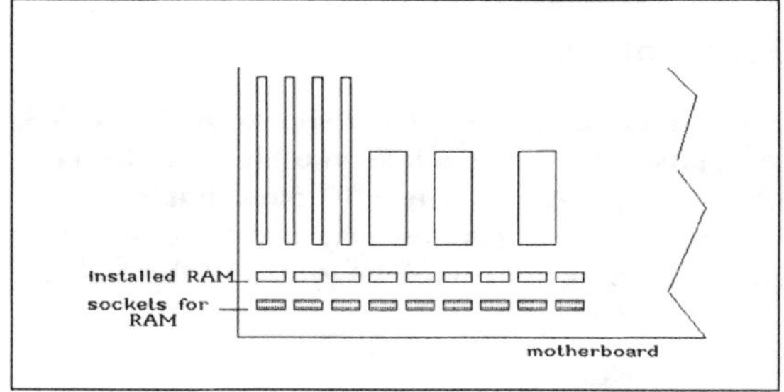

Figure 3.2   A typical set of chip sockets on the motherboard for adding extended memory in chip form: in this example, 9 x 1-Megabit chips. Your sockets might be laid out in a different pattern or a different part of the board.

visible (Figure 3.2). These sockets are usually numbered and have an indentation that should correspond with the Pin 1 end marker on each chip, so that you know which way round to insert the chips.

The only tools required are a Philips or Posidrive screwdriver and a pair of electrician's long-nosed pliers or, preferably, strong tweezers, which are needed to pull out some of the fastening screws.

You will need to buy the memory chips themselves unless you have already bought a kit. The types that are used depend on the machine; for an Amstrad PC1512 they are eighteen Type 4164 DRAMs rated at 150 ns or less. Each of these stores 64 Kbits per chip. To store 64 Kbits of bytes at 8 bits per byte requires eight of these chips, but since the PC uses an additional chip for the extra (parity) bit that is used for checking for valid data, nine chips are needed. Nine chips therefore provide 64 Kb and eighteen chips provide 128 Kb, bringing the total from 512 Kb to 640 Kb.

Other machines are likely to use either this set of 18 chips (now rather outdated and slow) or a set of more modern chips. Add-on memory boards are likely to use more modern chip types, and video graphics boards will probably use eight type 4464 chips. It is up to you to check that the type of chips are correct for your computer before buying them.

Preparation

Memory chips take the form shown in Figure 3.3, with pins arranged in a line on each side. The 4164 chips for the Amstrad use 16 pins, but chips intended for other upgrades may use more than this number; the 41464 uses 18 pins and the 514100 1-Mbit chips use 20 pins.

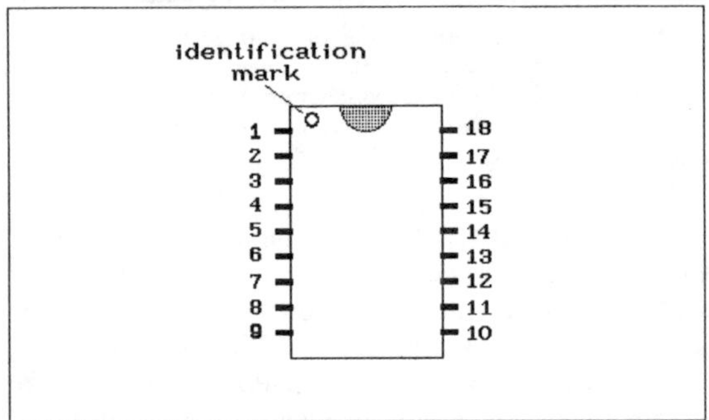

Figure 3.3 A typical memory chip shape, showing the identification marks for Pin 1. This is important, because the chip must be placed in the holder the correct way round. The example uses 18 pins; others have 20, 22 or 24 pins.

A memory chip, like any other type of chip, can be placed in either of two ways in its holder, and only one way is correct. Reversing the position of a chip in the holder is a certain way of damaging the chip electrically and since chips cannot be repaired this can be an expensive oversight.

- No damage will be done until the machine is switched on, however, so by careful inspection beforehand you can avoid such damage.

- Each chip has a mark which indicates the position of Pin 1, and the standard pattern of this mark (not observed by all manufacturers) is a hole of about 1 mm diameter and the same depth, placed next to Pin 1.

- Another marker is a rectangular notch placed at the Pin 1 end of the chip, and chips can be found with only the rectangular notch and no other marking. Whatever pattern is used, the end that contains Pin 1 will always be different from the other end.

- If a chip has a rectangular notch and several small circular depressions which could be taken for Pin 1 markers, the rectangular notch is the determining feature, and Pin 1 is the pin to the left of the notch when the chip is held as indicated in Figure 3.3.

Normally, the lines of chip holders are arranged so that the Pin 1 markers all face the same way, which is usually the same way as that of the chips already installed. Check carefully in case your machine deviates from this custom in any way.

The connecting pins of these chips are, in fact, flat ribbons of metal whose width is very narrow where they fit into the socket. This makes them fairly easy to bend.

- If each pin is not perfectly located into the socket, it is very likely that careless insertion will bend one or more pins under the chip instead of sliding into the receptacle, and the bent pins will not be visible, will not make contact, and will be very difficult to straighten.

- New holders are often rather stiff, so that a fair amount of force is needed to insert the chips – more than is needed, for example, to plug in a disk drive connecting cable.

- In addition, when an IC is delivered from the manufacturer, the pins are splayed out slightly, so that the chip does not fit easily into its socket. A few suppliers will offer chips whose pins are pre-bent for easier fitting and if you are unaccustomed to fitting chips this is a very useful luxury, as is an IC inserting tool.

To straighten one pin, hold the chip cupped in your hand so that you are touching all of the pins. If your hands are slightly moist the chances of damage from static are even more remote. With a pair of miniature metal pliers, hold the pin along its whole length and bend it into line. You will need to bend the pin rather further than is needed, because it will spring back slightly when it is released.

To bend a whole line of pins so that a chip with outward-bent pins will fit into a socket, put the chip down onto a flat wooden surface, lying on one line of pins. Hold the rest of the body of the chip in your fingers, and while pressing the row of pins firmly against the wooden surface, roll the chip slightly so that all of the pins are being bent inwards (Figure 3.4). Do this once for each row, and then check against the socket again.

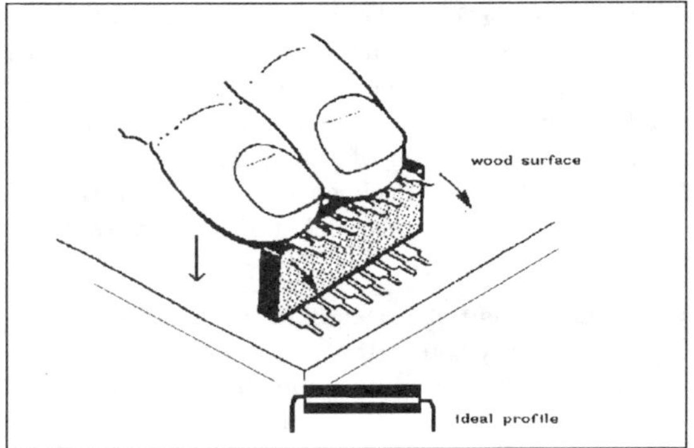

Figure 3.4   Bending the pins of a new chip slightly inwards to make it easier to fit the chip into its socket.

o One very good tip is to buy a spare socket of the correct type so that you can offer the chip up to this loose socket and check whether the pins are locating correctly with the socket slits. Firms such as Maplin Electronics or Cricklewood Electronics (see Appendix B) can supply such sockets and, if required, IC insertion and removal tools.

Repeat the bending procedure until the fit is perfect – remember that when you are fitting the chips into the sockets on the computer it will not be so easy to check that each pin is engaged.

If you overdo the bending and find that one row of pins is now bent inwards, you can reverse this by using a Bulldog clip to hold the row of pins and then bending them by pushing at the clip.

o There is a limit to the number of times that a pin can be bent to and fro without weakening and breaking, and you should try as far as possible to make sure that no pin is adjusted more than three times.

As it happens, the amount of bending that is needed is usually small, and the pins are sturdier than they look, so that there is a lot of leeway in this advice. This may seem tedious, but it makes insertion of the chips much simpler and greatly reduces the risk of bending a pin during insertion or, worse, of inserting a chip with one or more pins outside the socket. On a crowded board it can be very difficult to see one bent pin, and the only indication of trouble will be that the computer reports a memory fault when you eventually switch it on.

If you are likely to be upgrading more than one machine, or likely to make further upgrades that involve inserting chips, then a chip inserting tool is a worthwhile investment, and computer clubs will probably keep one that is available on loan.

● Try to avoid touching the pins. At one time, chips were very susceptible to damage by static electric discharge, but unless you are shuffling your feet on a nylon carpet and drawing sparks from everything you touch the risk to modern chips is very small.

● If you want to be ultra-safe, stand on a damp cotton mat, make sure that you lay chips on slightly damp paper, and wash your hands just before you handle chips so that your hands are slightly moist.

If you are making any other alterations such as adding a hard disk drive also, you should complete the memory expansion and test the machine thoroughly before adding anything else.

o Never make more than one modification at a
   time to any computer without testing fairly
   thoroughly.

Starting the installation

What you now need to look for is the jumper or DIL
switch whose setting will need to be changed so
that the machine can use the new memory. This
should be done before installing the memory so
that it is not forgotten later. Some machines may
require no alterations.

If by any unfortunate chance you find that you
have to abandon the expansion (because you have
damaged some chip pins, for example) the jumper
link or DIL switch will have to be reset, because it
must be set so as to show correctly the amount of
memory that is installed.

Once the chips have been prepared, they can be
inserted into the sockets.

1 Each chip should, in turn, be lined up, just rest-
   ing on its socket, ensuring that the chip is the
   correct way round and that its pins line up perfectly with the slits on the socket and are
   engaged with the slits.

2 When this has been done, the chip is inserted by
   gently pushing one end then the other, so that
   the chip is rocked into place with the wider parts
   of the pins hard against the socket. This usually
   leaves some space between the chip and the
   socket.

3 Quite a surprising amount of force is sometimes
   necessary, and unless the board that carries the
   sockets is unusually well supported it is advisable to place some sort of support under it –
   wooden blocks are very useful for this type of
   thing for a board lying out of the computer. You
   cannot support a motherboard in this way, however.

o Flexing the main circuit board excessively is something to be avoided as far as possible, because this can crack the narrow copper tracks that carry signals and voltages between chips, causing problems that can often be quite difficult to diagnose and cure.

The trouble here is that unless the machine is unusually well designed, you are almost certain to flex the motherboard to some extent in the course of plugging in anything from memory chips to expansion cards.

● It is sometimes easier to locate one line of pins in the holder, and then to exert some sideways force on the chip until the other line is engaged, then press in. This is usually needed because you cannot be certain that you have completely removed the splay from the pins.

● If you cannot line up the pins correctly with the socket without a great deal of force, do not attempt to insert the chip. Remove the chip and bend the pins in the way previously described until both lines fit easily into the socket. Testing with a spare socket, as noted earlier, is ideal.

● When you are pushing the chip home, watch for any pin bending, indicating that it is not fitting correctly into the socket.

Once you have inserted all the chips in this way, you can count yourself as now being reasonably experienced. Check again that all of the memory ICs are facing the correct way, and that the 512/640 link is in its 640 position. Look at the pins in a good light and preferably using a magnifying glass to check that no pins are bent and therefore not making contact.

You can now restore any cards you removed, check the interior once again, and replace the top of the casing.

● For old Amstrads and any other machines using a plastic casing, drop the retaining screws in and lightly turn them anticlockwise by hand. When you feel and hear the screw click, start turning clockwise. This ensures that you are using the same thread in the plastic as was used before.

● If you simply turn each screw you will probably cut another thread in the plastic, so that it will never hold securely again. Owners of low cost clones with flip top metal lids have none of this worry.

Reconnect the plugs and reconnect any other cables that were removed. Finally check everything and switch on. You should see the machine start up in its usual way, probably taking longer to boot up because of the extra memory that is being checked, but with the new amount of memory appearing in the screen notice. You can now try some of your favourite programs.

○ Try in particular any programs that report on the amount of memory used or remaining, so that you can be sure that the additional memory is being recognised (the sign-on message shows that the link is correctly set, but does not guarantee that the memory is working).

If there are memory problems, indicated by the memory count not including the added memory, or erratic behaviour and resetting to the A> or C> prompt, then it is possible that one of the new memory chips is faulty, that a pin is not making contact, or (unusually) that the new chips are not to the correct speed rating. Only after thorough checking to ensure that the added memory is working correctly should you try any other addition to the machine. Be sure to try out programs which make maximum use of the memory.

● Chips of too slow a speed rating may work while they are cold but start to give memory problems when they are hot. Some machines allow wait states to be added (using the CMOS Advanced Setup) to cope with slow chips, and if this cures the problem the solution is to retain the wait states or replace with faster chips.

Adding extended memory as chips

A large number of AT machines from only a few years ago were fitted with chips for 1 Mb of memory, but without sockets for SIMM or SIPP modules.

Such machines can have their extended memory added only by replacing all of the original chips with other types.

The most familiar pattern of this is the use of a set of 36 256 K chips in special holders (Figure 3.5), which can also hold wider 1 M chips with 20 pins rather than 18 pins per chip. By removing all of the 256 K chips and placing the 1 M chips into the outer lines of the sockets, the machine can then be upgraded from 1 Mb to 4 Mb.

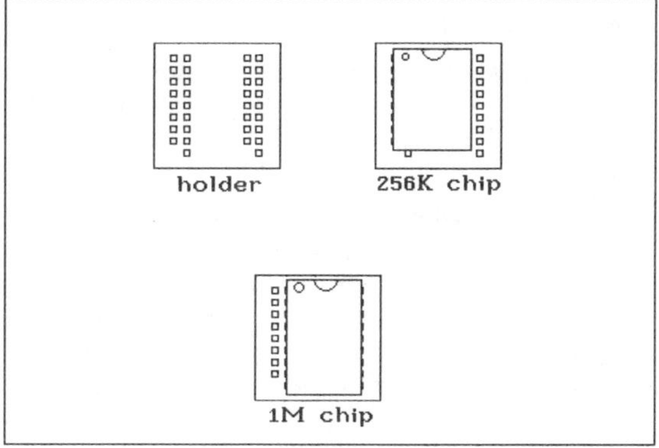

Figure 3.5 The special dual-purpose chip holders which are found in some older AT machines to allow an upgrade from 1 Mb to 4 Mb. All the 256 Kb chips have to be removed and the 1 Mb chips plugged into the alternative holder positions.

● Another scheme is to use 44256 chips (256 K of 4 bits) for main memory and 41256 (256 K of 1 bit) for parity.

● The most important point here is that you need to know if any alterations have to be made to jumpers or DIL switch settings. Unless you have some documentation to this effect, or can rely on notes passed from someone who has worked on an identical machine, do not attempt to change the chips. Many machines which used this method of expansion do not require any jumpers of switches to be altered, but you cannot be certain.

● You need to be able to remove the old chips – preferably intact, so that they can be used for other purposes if they are suitable.

● The most important point to make is that it is almost impossible to pull a chip straight out, using your fingers, without damaging either the chip or the board or both.

An IC removal tool is ideal, but if you do not have one, remove the chips as follows:

1 Insert two small screwdrivers, one under each end of the chip (Figure 3.6).

2 Start by gently turning one screwdriver blade so that the end of the chip will be raised slightly. This can be held while the other screwdriver is turned to raise the other end.

3 The first screwdriver can then be turned again, followed by the second until the chip can be raised no further. The screwdrivers can then be used as levers to lift the chip, one end at a time by no more than about 1 mm at a time until one end is released from the socket.

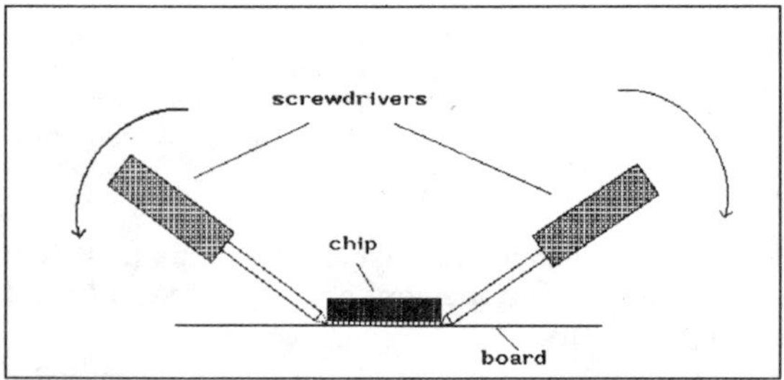

Figure 3.6 Using two screwdrivers to ease a chip out of its socket.

4 When this happens, hold the released end with one finger and use the remaining screwdriver to release the other end until you can lift the chip away. Do not attempt to lift the chip out if you encounter any resistance.

This method may appear to be slow, but it poses the least risk of damage to the chips and also to the board. The main practical problem is that if the chips are very tightly packed, there may not be room to insert the screwdrivers at a angle which allows them to be turned to lift the chip. There is no easy way round this short of making a tool like a miniature tack-lifter or using a commercial chip-removing tool, which is shaped like small tweezers with a hook at each end (Figure 3.7).

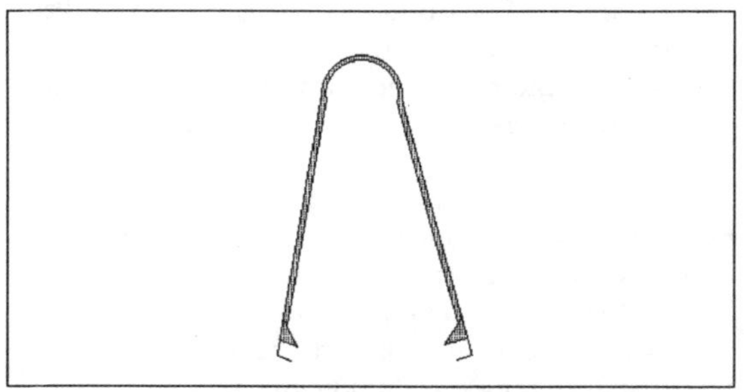

Figure 3.7   The shape of a simple commercial chip-removing tool. More elaborate chip removers can cost £20 or more.

As the old chips are removed, place them on a paper sheet (blotting paper is ideal because it is always slightly moist and electrically conductive). Now insert the new chips, using the methods described earlier. The chips will have come to you packed inside a plastic container, and this can now be used to house the old chips. Label the container to show that these are the old chips that you removed, and keep a note of the type number and speed of the old chips.

Adding memory by cards – mainly XT machines

The PC system provides a set of slot connectors into which expansion units in the form of plug-in circuit cards can be added, all housed within the main case of the machine. Computers of the PC type which have not followed this expansion scheme, or which have required other methods to be used, have had a short and ignoble life, because there is virtually nothing that you can do to expand them (and by this time no spare parts are available).

Conventional (base) memory can be expanded from 512 Kb to 640 Kb by using any of the large number of base fill-in cards which are available, either populated or unpopulated. There is very little saving in buying unpopulated cards if you also need to buy memory chips, and they are a bargain only if you happen to have a set of memory chips that will fit.

Expanding memory, whether conventional (base) memory, extended memory or expanded memory, by way of add-on cards, is neat and simple for the older XT and AT machines, and for a vast number of machines currently in production using 8088, 8086, 80286, 80386 or 80486 chips.

o 80286 and higher numbered chips are usually placed on motherboards that provide for adding extended memory directly, either as chips or, more likely now, by SIMM modules.

If the machine is described as using the XT or AT bus, it will take any of the huge number of expansion cards that are available – the only limitation is the number of expansion slots that the machine possesses. Many current models allow for as many as six expansion slots which, provided that these are free slots, are as many as you are ever likely to need. A few machines, however, have already used several slots for video card, hard-disk controller, serial/parallel port card and so on, leaving very few free for other uses.

- Before buying a computer, always check how many slots are free after the machine has been configured as you want it (if you request a hard disk, for example, this may require another controller card to be added).

- Most modern machines use a single card for IDE hard disk drive, floppy drive, parallel port and two serial ports, so that only a video card is needed for a complete machine, leaving four slots free in a six-slot machine.

- If memory can be added on the motherboard, always take this option, because the expansion slots on a PC are, in many, if not all, designs, run at a lower speed than the rest of the motherboard, making for slow access to any memory added in this way.

Note that some modern machines use very different bus structures. The IBM PS/2 machines use a bus structure called MCA (Micro-Channel Architecture). This results in the expansion slots for these machines being incompatible with those for the earlier machines, so that expansion cards for other machines cannot be used with PS/2.

An alternative form of bus, EISA, has been proposed by a group of other manufacturers, and a few machines with this structure have emerged. This type of machine uses slots into which the older cards can still be fitted, but these slots will also take cards which are designed to make more efficient use of the 80386 processor and deal with four-byte units of data.

- The majority of other PCs, however, retain the AT style of bus, also called ISA (Industry Standard Architecture) with its standardised slots into which the normal standard range of cards can be slotted.

The easiest way of showing how an expansion card is fitted is to go through an example, and the following is a description of fitting a Hyperam 286 EMS 4.0 board with 2 Mb of memory into an AT clone machine, the MATMOS AT. The details of the procedure will be different for XT machines and for

IBM Model 30; and obviously there will also be differences if you are using any other brand of board, such as an EEMS board. The methods, however, are much the same in outline.

The package for this example consists of the memory board itself together with two 5¼" floppies and one 3½" floppy. The 3½" disk contains all the software that is contained on the 5¼" disks (one disk almost filled, the other containing only the EMM.SYS file, which is the expanded memory manager – see Chapter 4.

- The software should, as always, be backed up before anything further is done. This should be to a disk or disks which are not write-protected – this is important, as writing will be done on the Install disk.

- The memory board is contained in plastic wrapping which is electrically conducting, and this should be retained. It is useful for laying the board onto while you are installing it, and for containing this or any other boards. Never throw this material away – it will quite certainly be useful some day.

Memory chips are much less vulnerable to static electricity when they are connected up on boards, but the fewer the risks you take the better. If you find that you are working on a day when shuffling your feet on the carpet will result in causing you a shock when you touch a radiator or other metal objects, or if you hear crackling noises when you rub your clothes then it is safer to work with moist hands and with your shoes off (and socks, unless they are cotton).

The Hyperam board caters for up to 8 Mb of memory arranged in pairs of banks. For 1 Mb, banks 0 and 1 should be filled with the slim TMS1024 chips and for 4 Mb banks 2 and 3 should also be filled. For 8 Mb, banks 4 to 7 must also be filled with chips. You should check the contents of your memory before proceeding. If you need to insert any more chips, this is the time to do so. Check with the manual for the board that you are using.

The next step, with the board still separate from the computer, is to start the INSTALL1 program from the disk(s). You are asked to enter the type of memory chips used, the number of banks filled and the EMS IO address. On the example, all of these entries were made as a default, using:

Type of memory chip	1Mbit
No. of banks filled	2 banks
EMS IO address	258

For the latter choices, keys F5 and F6 will cycle through the possible choices – leave the EMS address (used for access from DOS) at 258 unless you have other boards installed which might use this address number. Press the End key to record your answers or your acceptance of the existing answers, or the Esc key if you have decided not to proceed. You will be further asked if there are any more boards to install, and the default answer is No. The End and Esc keys can then be used with the same meanings as before.

You will then see a confirmation box showing, in this example, 2048 Kb of memory available and all assigned to expanded memory. You can assign some of this memory to system memory if your machine contains less than 640 Kb (otherwise leave this option as zero) and to extended memory if your machine and software can make good use of extended memory.

o Virtually all memory expansion boards will make use of software, and this example is typical of the type of questions that you will be asked. The alternative is a set of manuals showing how to set switches on the board.

The next message concerns the size of memory blocks that the board can release. On a 640 Kb machine this will normally be 64 Kb, and you will get a message showing this, and the address range: 64 Kb in size, of D000 to DFFF.

o You may see a different memory range recommended, depending on how your computer is configured. This range is shown in case there is a possibility of conflict with other hardware –

check that no other use of this address range is noted by using a memory audit program such as Manifest (see Chapter 4).

When you accept this setting, you are shown a diagram of the pattern into which the five switches on the board must be set. Figure 3.8 shows a typical diagram of this kind.

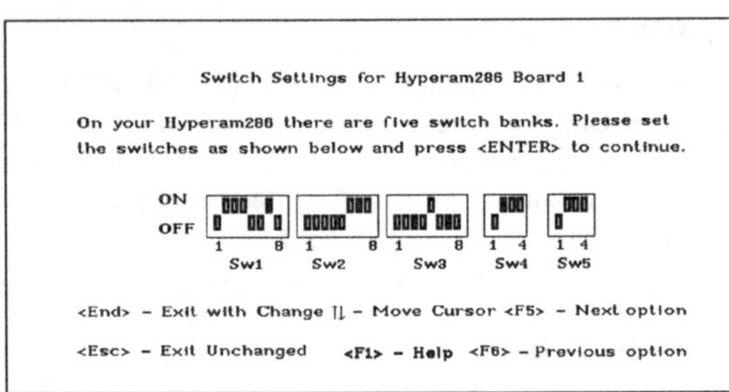

Figure 3.8 The form of diagram used to show settings for switches on a memory board.

- Check this diagram against the switches on the board, holding the board in its protective wrapping, and set the switches to match the pattern on the screen.

- Use the tip of a ball-pen to move the tiny switches – do not use a pencil because the point may break, leaving a trail of conducting graphite on the board. Press the Enter key to complete the first part of installation.

At this point, it's a good idea to check that no other switch settings are permissible. In fact, the Hyperam board allows the switch settings to be extended so as to increase the memory address range to obtain a 128 Kb window of memory.

The board is now ready to insert into the machine. Switch the computer off and leave it for at least five minutes to ensure that all of the power supplies in the computer have discharged. Remove the mains plug from the machine and install the board as follows:

1 Lift the cover and make sure that you have a 16-bit slot free. You may need to juggle with the positions of other boards to do this, particularly if you have in the past inserted an 8-bit board into a 16-bit slot. These 16-bit slots are about 5.5" long.

2 Unscrew the metal cover at the end of the slot which is at the rear of the computer, and lift the plate out – don't lose the small screw inside the machine.

3 Locate the EMS board into the slot, with the front end in the slotted guide and the plug-in part of the board engaging into the 16-bit slot. There will be resistance felt as you push the board down – make sure that it is aligned correctly so that the metal strip is lined over the hole for the securing screw.

4 Once the initial resistance is overcome, the board should push into place, and the retaining screw can be replaced – carefully to avoid losing it inside the case.

The lid can now be closed and the mains cable inserted again. When you switch on the machine there is a possibility that it may display some sort of memory message, requiring you (on an AT machine) to run the CMOS SETUP program (of the computer, not a program supplied with the board). If you used the memory board only to make the system memory up to 640 Kb and/or to increase extended memory, the installation is complete and you may need to run the CMOS SETUP to notify the enlarged expanded memory if this is noted in the CMOS.

If you are using the board to provide expanded memory, as is the sensible option on a 286 machine, then the request to use CMOS setup can usually be ignored, and if the machine has to be restarted it should proceed normally next time. The expanded memory software then has to be run in order to make use of the memory. For the Hyperam board, this program is INSTALL2. This *must* be run from the A: drive. You can select Quick Software Installation or Advanced Software Installation (or Exit).

Most users will opt for the Quick Installation. This starts by asking you if you want to allocate all of the Pool memory (on the board) to EMS, and for most users the answer will be Yes, the default (press the End key).

The next menu is titled Save Changes to Disk and consists of:

Display current Install state	Yes (Y/N)
Drive from which you normally boot	C (A or C)
Directory for Hypertec Drivers	\HYP\
Directory for Control Programs	\HYP\

The Installation Status display which follows should show the Pool Driver installed, but no Print Spooler, Ram Disk or Popup Menu (all parts of the Hyperam software which are installed if you opt for the Advanced Installation). These extras can be ignored unless you particularly need them. Finally, new CONFIG.SYS and AUTOEXEC.BAT files are written. The CONFIG.SYS file will have a new first line which is typically:

```
DEVICE= \HYP\POOL.SYS E2048 H258 (HRInstall)
```

In the AUTOEXEC.BAT file there will an addition in the PATH command (or a new line for PATH if you had none) which includes `C:\HYP (HRInstall)`.

Once all this is completed, you are ready to switch off and restart. You may get an error message about a non-standard disk when you restart, but this will appear only once, and you should see the expanded memory information appear (briefly) on the screen as the machine loads its software from the hard disk. For details of what you have gained, see the section on the use of Manifest in Chapter 4. The board described here behaved best when the selected memory area was C000 - DFFF, with the machine running the memory manager QEXT.SYS.

o The correct setting up of such a board is not the simplest of procedures, and not all expanded memory cards come with software that is so helpful.

Cards which have been fitted in this way become part of the computer, and if the card contains a ROM, this ROM will be addressed somewhere in the 768 K to 960 K region. When expanded memory is fitted to an XT type of machine, and the software has been correctly set up (which means that there will be a new DEVICE line placed very early on in the CONFIG.SYS file), you can make use of programs that are able to use expanded memory.

o Remember, however, that expanded memory will normally be accessed in 64 Kb chunks, corresponding to the 64 K of address numbers that happen to be free.

When you use an expanded memory board to EEMS standards, it is possible to make use of expanded memory in larger units. The snag, however, is that the only way of obtaining sufficient address numbers is by switching out memory on the main board, something that is hard to accept.

o If, for example, your machine allows you to switch out 128 Kb of memory on the main board, so that the main board has only 512 Kb left, you can then use larger pieces of expanded memory at a time.

This is very seldom acceptable nowadays, so that modern methods of making use of additional memory for AT machines concentrate on the use of extended memory, using this either directly by way of front-end programs such as Windows 3.0 or 3.1 or by way of software which can use the extended memory as if it were expanded memory (in 64 Kb pieces).

o Expanded memory is now an option that should be used only for XT machines, remembering that what you spend expanding the memory might better be used in buying a more modern machine.

Even when you have successfully installed an expanded or extended memory board your troubles may not be over, because the software of some boards conflicts with MS-DOS 5.0. In particular, the installation program for the popular Intel Aboveboard, tests the memory in a way that corrupts extended memory if it is in use at the time.

- Before you install the software for Aboveboard, reboot the machine from a floppy that does not load in any software such as SMARTDrive or a RAMdisk that makes use of extended memory.

- There are no further problems once the Aboveboard installation is complete.

Adding extended memory

A few machines provide for adding extended memory in the form of 1 M memory chips, using eight or nine chips in holders on the motherboard. Usually only another 1 Mb can be fitted in this way, and the more recent machines have chips on the motherboard only for the main first 1 Mb of memory.

o The much more common method of fitting extended memory on the motherboard is by way of SIMM or SIPP units.

SIMM means Single In-line Memory Module, and is like a miniature expansion card containing a set of memory chips. Connections are made to the SIMM just as they are to expansion cards, using an edge connector, a set of tiny metal tongues on the card which engage in springs on the holder. The SIPP differs from the SIMM only in using a line of pins rather than the edge connector; the name means Single In-line Pin Podule. The SIMM units (Figure 3.9) are more common nowadays.

The SIMM units are inserted into their holders with the metal tongues on the SIMM pressing against the metal contact of the holder. SIPP units are usually marked, and the holders should show the identification lettering at the Pin 1 end. In general, SIPPs are often poorly marked and it is

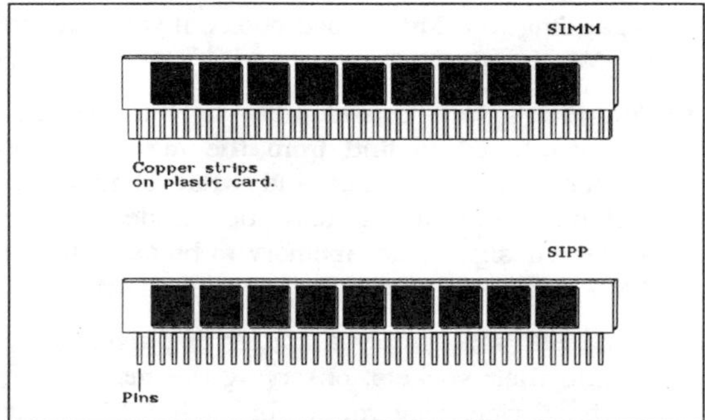

Figure 3.9 The shape of typical SIMM and SIPP units, which can carry large amounts of RAM without the need to insert individual chips. SIMMs are more common for extending memory, SIPPs are usually found built in by the manufacturer.

much more common to use SIMMs for expansion, with SIPPs fitted by the manufacturer.

- The standard SIMM and SIPP units are 1 M x 8, 1 M x 9, 4 M x 8 and 4 M x 9, allowing for expansion by 1 Mb or 4 Mb per unit. Some manufacturers provide 2 M x 8, 2 M x 9 and even 16 M x 8 and 16 M x 9 SIMMs. You will have to check with the manual for your machine to find which size of SIMMs it can use – the usual selection is 1 M x 9 or 4 M x 9.

- This does not mean that you can expand a 1 Mb computer to 2 Mb by adding a 1 Mb SIMM. The usual arrangement is that SIMM or SIPP units must be installed in twos, so that you can expand by 2 Mb at a time using the 1 Mb SIMMs and by 8 Mb at a time using the 4 Mb SIMMs. Check with the manual for your computer to find what arrangement is needed. Some machines may even require SIMMs to be installed in sets of four.

- If, using the two-SIMM system, you want your computer to contain only 2 Mb of RAM, you install two 1 Mb SIMMs and remove the original 1 Mb chips from the motherboard. Most users will prefer to add the SIMMs and retain the chips, so expanding to 3 Mb (a good choice if you want to run Windows).

- Computers vary considerably in this respect, and you need to find from the manual what memory can be added and what changes to switches or jumpers may be needed. Some modern designs allow memory to be extended in 2 Mb units with no change to jumper settings.

Fitting SIPPs is simply a matter of plugging the units into their sockets, observing the marks that show the correct way round for each SIPP. Early types of SIMM sockets were also built rather like expansion card slots, so that the SIMM unit was pushed straight into the socket.

- The more modern SIMM holder is more elaborate. The SIMM is slotted in at an angle of about 45° and then straightened up, when two plastic clips hold it in place. This locking arrangement is very much more secure than the older type, and takes the same SIMM units.

- You must be certain which type of holder your computer uses; machines made up to the first half of 1991 were still using the straight push-in type of SIMM holder, though some manufacturers had switched over. By 1992, the slide in and twist type was predominant. It is important not to use the wrong method of insertion as this could damage the SIMM units and possibly the holders also.

Adding RAM to boards

The addition of RAM to memory boards that come unpopulated or with a small amount of RAM is done using the same choice of chips or SIMMs as for motherboards. The chips that are used are sometimes types that are now seldom seen on motherboards, and quite often the speed rating will be low (access times of 100 ns or more). This is because the bus signals on the motherboard are usually slower than at the microprocessor: a common figure is one sixth of the microprocessor clock speed.

Adding RAM to VGA graphics boards usually requires chips that are definitely no longer used on motherboards, and also fairly slow. Remember that it does no harm (apart from a slight sting in the wallet) to use faster memory than is required, but using slower memory that is required can cause a lot of trouble.

o As always, you have to study any documentation you have with considerable care, and to check by examining the board itself, because documentation is, unfortunately, not always accurate. The shape of a board, for example, may be changed after the documentation has been printed.

Graphics boards are usually very easy to upgrade, with the positions of the chips being shown clearly and the type also marked on the board. You should, however, query why you want to increase the memory of a VGA board.

o Almost certainly, you will do this so that you can run the higher resolution Super VGA (SVGA) graphics modes.

SVGA modes not only require more memory, they run slower and require additional driver programs in the PC for each program that will use them. You may find that few of your existing programs contain drivers for such boards, or that the types of boards for which you have drivers do not include the board you want to use.

● Check that the programs, which are usually drawing or painting programs, that you want to use with SVGA, contain a driver for the board you are using. Do not assume that this will be provided or that one for a different type of board will work.

● Some SVGA video boards which are not among the well-known makes (Figure 3.10) will come with their own software drivers. The snag is that these will be for a limited range of programs (one for each program) and that your favourite programs will not be included.

Amdek : VGA ADAPTER/132
AST: VGA Plus
ATI: VIP
ATI: VGA Wonder
Compaq: VGC Board
Genoa: VGA
Orchid: Designer VGA
Orchid: Designer VGA, 800 x 600
Orchid: Pro Designer Plus
Paradise: VGA Plus
Paradise: VGA Plus 16
Paradise: VGA Pro
Sigma Designs: SigmaVGA
STB: VGA Extra EM
Tecmar: VGA
Tecmar: VGA AD
Video-7: FastWrite
Video-7: V RAM VGA
Willow: VGA-TV/Publisher's
Willow: VGA-TV + Genlock

Figure 3.10 The major names of SVGA graphics boards for which software drivers are readily available – this is a typical set recognised by De Luxe Paint-II.

● Programs such as Windows make very intensive use of graphics, and using SVGA will slow down Windows – never a desirable option (see Chapters 4 and 5).

4 Making Use of Memory

Memory reports

Whether you have added memory or are about to, a report on the current state of memory is useful and revealing, and there are several utilities which provide such reports. Of these, the most common, because it is supplied along with MS-DOS 5.0, is MEM. There is also a MEM utility supplied as part of DR-DOS 6.0 which provides similar information (though with more facilities and a better format of report).

Using MS-DOS MEM in its simplest form gives the information typically illustrated in Figure 4.1 for a 286 machine from Micro Surgeons (Isenstein) Ltd. This is a report on the main (system) memory, showing that the conventional memory is 655360 bytes (640 Kb), of which some 584976 bytes (571.26 Kb) is available for programs.

o In this example, there is a large amount of conventional memory available because much of MS-DOS 5.0 has been relocated to the first 64 Kb of extended memory. DR-DOS 6.0 can similarly have its command program relocated.

The part of the report dealing with extended memory looks rather confusing at first sight. The machine is fitted with a total of 2 Mb of RAM memory, and the report from MEM shows 1048576 (1 Mb) of contiguous extended memory, meaning memory with addresses in consecutive series without breaks. None of this memory is shown as being *available contiguous extended memory*.

o This is because Available Contiguous Extended Memory has a restricted meaning – it means memory that is not being managed by some utility such as HIMEM.SYS. In this example, all of the extended memory is under HIMEM.SYS management and being used in this example for the SMARTDrive cache program, so that none is left for any other uses.

```
Address      Name        Size      Type
--------     --------     ------    ------
000000                    000400    Interrupt Vector
000400                    000100    ROM Communication Area
000500                    000200    DOS Communication Area

000700       IO           000A60    System Data

001160       MSDOS        0013D0    System Data

002530       IO           001A60    System Data
             SETVER       000190    DEVICE=
             HIMEM        000430    DEVICE=
             HHSCAND      0009A0    DEVICE=
                          0005D0    FILES=
                          000100    FCBS=
                          000200    BUFFERS=
                          0001C0    LASTDRIVE=
003FA0       MSDOS        000040    System Program

003FF0       COMMAND      000940    Program
004940       COMMAND      000040    Data
004990       COMMAND      000100    Environment
004AA0       KEYCLICK     000080    Environment
004B30       DOSKEY       001020    Program
005B60       KEYCLICK     000150    Program
005CC0       MARK         000080    Environment
005D50       MOUSE        004250    Program
009FB0       MARK         000540    Program
00A500       CATCH        000080    Environment
00A590       CATCH        001B30    Program
00C0D0       DOSSHELL     000080    Environment
00C160       DOSSHELL     000800    Program
00C970       COMMAND      000080    Data
00CA00       COMMAND      000200    Environment
00CC10       MSDOS        000050    -- Free --
00CC70       PINCH        000080    Environment
00CD00       COMMAND      000050    Data
00CD60       MEM          000080    Environment
00CDF0       MSDOS        0007C0    -- Free --
00D5C0       PINCHF12     000080    Environment
00D650       PINCHF12     0014F0    Program
00EB50       MSDOS        000940    -- Free --
00F4A0       PINCH        0014E0    Program
010990       COMMAND      000940    Program
0112E0       MEM          0176F0    Program
0289E0       MSDOS        077610    -- Free --


   655360 bytes total conventional memory
   655360 bytes available to MS-DOS
   584976 largest executable program size

  1048576 bytes total contiguous extended memory
        0 bytes available contiguous extended memory
   983040 bytes available XMS memory
        -  MS-DOS resident in High Memory Area
```

Figure 4.1   The MS-DOS MEM report from a 286 machine, using the basic format of MEM.

In addition, 983040 (960 Kb) is shown as available XMS memory, meaning that this can be used by any program that requires extended memory in XMS form. This is the form of extended memory that HIMEM.SYS delivers. At the time of writing, apart from Windows 3.0 and 3.1, only Lotus 1-2-3 version 3.1 and DisplayWrite used memory of this format, and Lotus 1-2-3 also requires some expanded memory (see Appendix D).

- Programs such as SMARTDrive and RAMdisk can optionally use extended memory.

- This XMS memory is shown as available because this is the memory controlled by HIMEM.SYS, and SMARTDrive can release some of this memory if it is required by a program, in particular by Windows 3.0 or 3.1.

Using MEM with switch commands

By typing MEM /P as a command, information is made available on the amount of memory being used by programs. This is a much more extensive list (Figure 4.2), showing in detail how parts of the memory are used.

- In this example, the only programs that exist in the memory, apart from MS-DOS itself, are the utilities loaded by AUTOEXEC.BAT. These are memory-resident and will remain in place until the machine is switched off (see Chapter 2 for details of how to remove memory-resident programs).

- The address numbers are shown in hexadecimal, the programmers' counting system (see Appendix A).

As a guide, numbers in this list that start with 00 are in the first 64 Kb of memory, those starting with 01 are in the second 64 Kb segment, and numbers starting with 02 are in the third 64 Kb segment. The tenth segment uses 0A (using A to mean 10). The conventional 640 Kb corresponds to ten segments of 64 Kb each. Each number refers to a 64 Kb segment of memory.

For each program in the memory, an environment space and a program space is shown. The *environment space* is the memory that the program might need to use for information on commands, and it typically contains any PATH and option details. The environment space for most programs is 128 bytes (80 in hexadecimal), and is not used to any extent

```
Address        Name         Size       Type
-------        --------     ------     ------
000000                      000400     Interrupt Vector
000400                      000100     ROM Communication Area
000500                      000200     DOS Communication Area

000700         IO           000A60     System Data
               CON                       System Device Driver
               AUX                       System Device Driver
               PRN                       System Device Driver
               CLOCK$                    System Device Driver
               A: - C:                   System Device Driver
               COM1                      System Device Driver
               LPT1                      System Device Driver
               LPT2                      System Device Driver
               LPT3                      System Device Driver
               COM2                      System Device Driver
               COM3                      System Device Driver
               COM4                      System Device Driver

001160         MSDOS        0013D0     System Data

002530         IO           001A60     System Data
               SETVER       000190       DEVICE=
               SETVERXX                    Installed Device Driver
               HIMEM        000430       DEVICE=
               XMSXXXX0                    Installed Device Driver
               HHSCAND      0009A0       DEVICE=
               HH$SCAN                     Installed Device Driver
                            0005D0       FILES=
                            000100       FCBS=
                            000200       BUFFERS=
                            0001C0       LASTDRIVE=
003FA0         MSDOS        000040     System Program

003FF0         COMMAND      000940     Program
004940         COMMAND      000040     Data
004990         COMMAND      000100     Environment
004AA0         KEYCLICK     000080     Environment
004B30         DOSKEY       001020     Program
005B60         KEYCLICK     000150     Program
005CC0         MARK         000080     Environment
005D50         MOUSE        004250     Program
009FB0         MARK         000540     Program
00A500         CATCH        000080     Environment
00A590         CATCH        001B30     Program
00C0D0         DOSSHELL     000080     Environment
00C160         DOSSHELL     000800     Program
00C970         COMMAND      000080     Data
00CA00         COMMAND      000200     Environment
00CC10         MSDOS        000050     -- Free --
00CC70         PINCH        000080     Environment
00CD00         COMMAND      000050     Data
00CD60         MEM          000080     Environment
00CDF0         MSDOS        0007C0     -- Free --
00D5C0         PINCHF12     000080     Environment
00D650         PINCHF12     0014F0     Program
00EB50         MSDOS        000940     -- Free --
00F4A0         PINCH        0014E0     Program
010990         COMMAND      000940     Program
0112E0         MEM          0176F0     Program
0289E0         MSDOS        077610     -- Free --


   655360 bytes total conventional memory
   655360 bytes available to MS-DOS
   584976 largest executable program size

  1048576 bytes total contiguous extended memory
        0 bytes available contiguous extended memory
   983040 bytes available XMS memory
          MS-DOS resident in High Memory Area
```

Figure 4.2 The more extensive report from MEM /P.

in the small utilities that are loaded in the examples here.

Using MEM /D produces a similar display, but with
more details of the use of memory blocks. This option is not intended for the average PC user, more
for the programmer who needs to know about
memory use. Using MEM /C produces a list that is
easier to understand, with addresses in conventional (denary) forms as well as in hexadecimal (Figure
4.3).

```
Conventional Memory :

  Name                Size in Decimal        Size in Hex
-----------------   ----------------------   --------------
  MSDOS               12288      ( 12.0K)        3000
  SETVER                400      (  0.4K)         190
  HIMEM                1072      (  1.0K)         430
  HHSCAND              2464      (  2.4K)         9A0
  COMMAND              2688      (  2.6K)         A80
  KEYCLICK              464      (  0.5K)         1D0
  DOSKEY               4128      (  4.0K)        1020
  MARK                 1472      (  1.4K)         5C0
  MOUSE               16976      ( 16.6K)        4250
  CATCH                7088      (  6.9K)        1BB0
  DOSSHELL             2176      (  2.1K)         880
  COMMAND              3088      (  3.0K)         C10
  PINCH                5472      (  5.3K)        1560
  PINCHF12             5488      (  5.4K)        1570
  FREE                   80      (  0.1K)          50
  FREE                 2128      (  2.1K)         850
  FREE                 2368      (  2.3K)         940
  FREE               584976      (571.3K)       8ED10

Total  FREE :        589552      (575.7K)

Total bytes available to programs :              589552    (575.7K)
Largest executable program size :                584976    (571.3K)

  1048576 bytes total contiguous extended memory
        0 bytes available contiguous extended memory
   983040 bytes available XMS memory
          MS-DOS resident in High Memory Area
```

*Figure 4.3 The report from MEM /C, which shows a list
of programs in memory, using denary address numbers
as well as hexadecimal.*

o If you have loaded any programs other than MS-
   DOS into high memory you can expect to find
   hexadecimal address numbers starting with 09,
   0A, 0B, 0C, 0D and 0E for these high memory
   addresses. Numbers starting with 1 (not 01) are
   in the second megabyte of (extended) memory.

The DR-DOS MEM command in its simplest form
provides the display shown in Figure 4.4, this time
for a 386SX machine (a Micro Surgeons Swift) being

Memory Type	Total Bytes (Kbytes)		Available	
Conventional	655,360 (	640K)	642,208 (	627K)
Upper	188,416 (	184K)	33,312 (	32K)
High	65,520 (	64K)	6,325 (	6K)
Extended	393,216 (	384K)	0 (	0K)
Extended via XMS	N/A		139,264 (	136K)
EMS	180,224 (	176K)	98,304 (	96K)

Figure 4.4   The DR-DOS MEM report from a 386 machine with only 1 Mb of RAM.

installed. Since this uses a 386 processor, DR-DOS allows its EMM386 memory driver to be used, and this permits the use of extended memory as EMS expanded memory.

o Once again, though, the display is confusing because the figures do not add up in any simple way. This is because the areas of memory in the Total column overlap. For example, all the allocations to Upper, High, XMS and EMS in this case must be made from the extended memory, which in this case is only 384 Kb (the machine had not been fitted with further extended memory at that time).

Using MEM /B with DR-DOS produces the display shown in Figure 4.5. This shows how the DR-DOS operating system makes use of the memory, using comparatively small and scattered pieces.

Address	Owner	Size		Type
0:0000	--------	400h,	1,024	Interrupt vectors
40:0000	--------	100h,	256	ROM BIOS data area
50:0000	DR DOS	200h,	512	DOS data area
70:0000	DR BIOS	B20h,	2,848	Device drivers
122:1000	DR DOS	11B0h,	4,528	System
23D:0000	DR DOS	B60h,	2,912	System
2F3:0000	COMMAND	210h,	528	Program
314:0000	COMMAND	210h,	528	Environment
335:0000	MEM	80h,	128	Environment
33D:0000	MEM	13AE0h,	80,608	Program
16EB:0000	--------	89150h,	561,488	FREE

Figure 4.5 The DR-DOS MEM /B report, which is better.

The MEM /D command of DR-DOS 6.0 produces the display of device drivers (Figure 4.6), some of which are built in by the operating systems, others are loaded in by the CONFIG.SYS file. In this list, the EMM386 driver is used for managing the ex-

```
- Address ----- Owner ----- Size -----------  - Type -
    70:050B   PRN                               Built-in device driver
    70:051D   LPT1                              Built-in device driver
    70:052F   LPT2                              Built-in device driver
    70:0541   LPT3                              Built-in device driver
    70:0553   AUX                               Built-in device driver
    70:0565   COM1                              Built-in device driver
    70:0577   COM2                              Built-in device driver
    70:0589   COM3                              Built-in device driver
    70:059B   COM4                              Built-in device driver
    70:0602   CLOCK$                            Built-in device driver
    70:0645   CON                               Built-in device driver
    70:0671      A:-C:                          Built-in device driver
   122:0048   NUL                               Built-in device driver
   24F:0000   EMMXXXX0       640h,    1,600     Loadable device driver
  E302:0000   SMARTAAR       2D0h,      720     Loadable device driver
```

Figure 4.6   Using DR-DOS MEM /D to show device drivers.

tended memory of the 386 machine and SMAR-TAAR (a comment of some kind, perhaps) is a cache program for Microsoft Windows.

The MEM /M command provides a list of memory limits with a visual display (Figure 4.7). This is particularly useful for a 386 machine in which some of the memory between the 640 Kb limit and the end of memory (at 1 Mb in this unexpanded machine) can be used for loading parts of the DOS system and utilities.

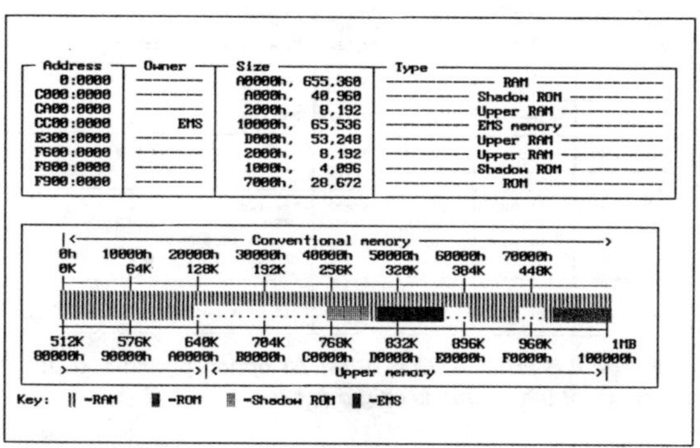

Figure 4.7   Using DR-DOS MEM /M to provide a report on the use of memory.

Finally, MEM /A will provide a combined display, the first part of which (Figure 4.8) is a very useful summary of memory use.

Address	Owner	Size		Type
0:0000	--------	A0000h,	655,360	-------------- RAM ----------------
0:0000	--------	400h,	1,024	Interrupt vectors
40:0000	--------	100h,	256	ROM BIOS data area
50:0000	DR DOS	200h,	512	DOS data area
70:0000	DR BIOS	B20h,	2,848	Device drivers
70:050B	PRN			Built-in device driver
70:051D	LPT1			Built-in device driver
70:052F	LPT2			Built-in device driver
70:0541	LPT3			Built-in device driver
70:0553	AUX			Built-in device driver
70:0565	COM1			Built-in device driver
70:0577	COM2			Built-in device driver
70:0589	COM3			Built-in device driver
70:059B	COM4			Built-in device driver
70:0602	CLOCK$			Built-in device driver
70:0645	CON			Built-in device driver
70:0671	A:-C:			Built-in device driver
122:0000	DR DOS	11B0h,	4,528	System
122:0048	NUL			Built-in device driver
23D:0000	DR DOS	B60h,	2,912	System
24F:0000	EMMXXXX0	640h,	1,600	Loadable device driver
2F3:0000	COMMAND	210h,	528	Program
314:0000	COMMAND	210h,	528	Environment
335:0000	MEM	80h,	128	Environment
33D:0000	MEM	13AE0h,	80,608	Program
16EB:0000	--------	89140h,	561,472	FREE
9FFF:0000	EXCLUDED	2A010h,	172,048	Upper system memory
C000:0000	--------	A000h,	40,960	---------- Shadow ROM ------------
CA00:0000	--------	2000h,	8,192	---------- Upper RAM -------------
CA00:0000	DR DOS	1330h,	4,912	System
CB33:0000	SUPERPCK	30h,	48	Environment
CB36:0000	--------	C90h,	3,216	FREE
CBFF:0000	EXCLUDED	17010h,	94,224	Upper system memory
CC00:0000	EMS	10000h,	65,536	---------- EMS memory -----------
DC00:0000	EMM386	7000h,	28,672	EMM386 device driver code
E300:0000	--------	D000h,	53,248	---------- Upper RAM -------------
E300:0000	DR DOS	2F0h,	752	System
E302:0000	SMARTAAR	2D0h,	720	Loadable device driver
E32F:0000	SUPERPCK	7770h,	30,576	Program
EAA6:0000	--------	5590h,	21,904	FREE
EFFF:0000	EXCLUDED	6010h,	24,592	Upper system memory
F600:0000	--------	2000h,	8,192	---------- Upper RAM -------------
F600:0000	--------	2000h,	8,192	FREE
F800:0000	--------	1000h,	4,096	---------- Shadow ROM -----------
F900:0000	--------	7000h,	28,672	-------------- ROM -----------------
FFFF:00E0	COMMAND	1380h,	4,992	Program
FFFF:1470	--------	120h,	288	FREE
FFFF:1590	DR DOS	DE0h,	3,552	DR DOS BIOS code
FFFF:2370	DR DOS	9440h,	37,952	DR DOS kernel code
FFFF:B7B0	--------	1795h,	6,037	FREE
FFFF:CF45	KEYB	11CBh,	4,555	Program
FFFF:E110	DR DOS	1E00h,	7,680	15 Disk buffers

Figure 4.8 The DR-DOS MEM /A option provides a full report, of which this is only a portion.

o A peculiarity of the MEM command of DR-DOS is that, though it can be used with MS-DOS, it will lock up under MS-DOS if you specify an option letter that is not available. You will need to reboot to regain control.

Windows MSD

Windows 3.1 contains MSD, a method of analysing the hardware and resident software of a machine very thoroughly. MSD is intended to make it easier for Microsoft technical staff to analyse compatibility problems, but the file it produces on a machine can just as easily be used by any owner as a way of finding out how memory is used, particularly the memory in the range of 640 Kb to 1024 Kb.

The program is run from MS-DOS by finding the Windows directory and running MSD (which does not require Windows to be running).

○ You can opt for a screen view only, a printout or a file output, and the file output is particularly useful as it allows you to view and print later as you wish. The file is called REPORT.MSD and it starts with your name and other identifying material, followed by a system overview report (Figure 4.9).

```
----------------------- Summary Information -------------------------
                    Computer: Unknown/Unknown, 80286
                      Memory: 640K, 1024K Ext
                       Video: VGA, Quadtel, 512
                     Network: No Network
                  OS Version: MS-DOS 5.00, DOSSHELL
                       Mouse: Serial Mouse 8.20
              Other Adapters: Game Adapter
                 Disk Drives: A: B: C:
                   LPT Ports: 1
                   COM Ports: 2

-------------------------- Computer ---------------------------------
         Computer Name: Unknown
        Computer Model:
     BIOS Manufacturer: Unknown
          BIOS Version: right 1989, 1990 Quadtel Corp. Version 3.00 All r
                        yright 1987-1990 Quadtel Corp. Version 3.05.01 Al
                        ght 1987-1990 Quadtel Corp. Version 3.05.01 All R
         BIOS Category: IBM PC/AT
         BIOS ID Bytes: FC 01 00
             BIOS Date: 06/02/90
             Processor: 80286
       Math Coprocessor: None
              Keyboard: Enhanced
              Bus Type: ISA/AT/Classic Bus
        DMA Controller: Yes
         Cascaded IRQ2: Yes
      BIOS Data Segment: None
```

Figure 4.9 The MSD report file starts with a system overview useful if you need to know these details of the system.

The most useful part of the analysis then follows (Figure 4.10). This deals with how the first megabyte of memory above the 640 Kb mark is used, and unusually it starts at the highest address of 1024 Kb, FFFFF in hexadecimal.

```
------------------------------------- Memory -------------------------------------

   Legend:  Available "  "  RAM "##"  ROM "RR"  Possibly Available ".."
      EMS Page Frame "PP"  Used UMBs "UU"  Free UMBs "FF"


 1024K FC00 RRRRRRRRRRRRRRRR FFFF  Conventional Memory
       F800 RRRRRRRRRRRRRRRR FBFF                Total: 640K
       F400 RRRRRRRRRRRRRRRR F7FF            Available: 530K
  960K F000 RRRRRRRRRRRRRRRR F3FF                       543504 bytes
       EC00 ................ EFFF
       E800 ................ EBFF  Extended Memory
       E400 ................ E7FF                Total: 1024K
  896K E000 ................ E3FF
       DC00 ................ DFFF  XMS Information
       D800 ................ DBFF           XMS Version: 2.00
       D400 ................ D7FF        Driver Version: 2.77
  832K D000 ................ D3FF      A20 Address Line: Enabled
       CC00 ................ CFFF      High Memory Area: In use
       C800 ................ CBFF             Available: 0K
       C400 RRRRRRRRRRRRRRRR C7FF    Largest Free Block: 0K
  768K C000 RRRRRRRRRRRRRRRR C3FF
       BC00 ................ BFFF
       B800 ................ BBFF
       B400 ################ B7FF
  704K B000 ################ B3FF
       AC00 ................ AFFF
       A800 ................ ABFF
       A400 ................ A7FF
  640K A000 ................ A3FF
```

Figure 4.10 The MSD analysis for the first Mb of memory.

o In this analysis, **R** is used to indicate use by a ROM, # means RAM present and dots indicate addresses that are not detected as being in use. There are also codings for addresses used by EMS and by UMB controllers.

Each block of memory is shown as a line representing 16 Kb, with the starting segment address on the left and the ending segment address on the right.

In this part of the report, the area shown as having RAM in address number starting at 768 Kb is the RAM for the video card. An analysis of the video card information follows, but without details of the use of memory since this is standard for this type of card. A lot of the following parts of the report are, as is inevitable, technical since they are intended for Microsoft personnel, but the report on TSR programs (Figure 4.11) is revealing.

```
--------------------------- TSR Programs ---------------------------

Program Name          Address   Size    Command Line Parameters
-------------------   -------   ------   ------------------------------------
System Data            0253      6864
  SETVER              0255       400    SETVERXX
  HIMEM               026F      1184    XMSXXXX0
  HHSCAND             02BA      2464    HH$SCAN
  File Handles        0355      1488
  FCBS                03B3       256
  BUFFERS             03C4       512
  Directories         03E5       448
System Code            0401        64
COMMAND.COM            0406      2368
Free Memory            049B        64
COMMAND.COM            04A0       256
SMARTDRV.EXE           04B1        64    A- B- 512 /q
SMARTDRV.EXE           04B6     25728    A- B- 512 /q
KEYCLICK.COM           0AFF       128
KEYCLICK.COM           0B08      4128    /insert
KEYCLICK.COM           0C0B       336
MARK.COM               0C21       128
MARK.COM               0C2A     16976
MARK.COM               1050      1344
DOSSHELL.exe           10A5       128    :\MSDOS\DOSSWAP.EXE
DOSSHELL.exe           10AE      4448    :\MSDOS\DOSSWAP.EXE
DOSSWAP.EXE            11C5       128
DOSSWAP.EXE            11CE     35600
???                    1A80       128
COMMAND.COM            1A89      2368
paramete               1B1E       512
???                    1B3F        80
MSD.EXE                1B45       128
MSD.EXE                1B4E    291648
MSD.EXE                6283      8192
MSD.EXE                6484     10032
Free Memory            66F8       544
Free Memory            671B    233024
```

Figure 4.11 The MSD report on TSR programs in the memory.

Note that MSD counts its own very substantial presence. This machine has been using the most recent version of SMARTDrive (as supplied with Windows 3.1) which takes up much more memory space than earlier versions. There is also a printout of the CONFIG.SYS and AUTOEXEC.BAT files, plus any WINDOWS initialising files (such as WIN.INI).

Using Manifest

Manifest is a program from Quarterdeck UK, programmers of DesqView, which provides information about your computer – possibly more than you want to know at this stage.

o The importance of Manifest is that it will tell you very clearly how much memory is available for various purposes, and how much is in use.

Manifest is supplied along with the memory managing programs QEMM386 (for 386 or 486 machines) or QRAM (for 286, 8088 and 8086 machines). For these older machines QRAM will make odd pieces of memory available for use; QEMM will carry out the same type of actions for 386 and 486 machines. The following illustrations have been prepared on the Swift 25 MHz 386SX machine before expanding it from 1 Mb to 5 Mb RAM.

- Note that the old Version 1.0 of Manifest cannot be used along with MS-DOS 5.0, and an upgrade will be needed if you have this version. Even some later versions can lock up in certain conditions when used with MS-DOS 5.0.

- The use of Manifest in analysing memory use is part of what Quarterdeck call *memory account-ancy*, a matter of finding out how memory is used and trying to use it better.

Manifest can be installed quite separately from DESQview if you are not using DESQview, or it can be run under DESQview like any other program. When Manifest runs, it uses the F1 and F2 keys for its own purposes:

1 The F1 key summons Help on the data that is being displayed by Manifest.

2 The F2 key allows printing of the Manifest reports. When you use F2 you are presented with a useful set of options.

3 You can opt to print to the printer or to a new file, or to add the information to an existing file. If you opt for a New File, the suggested name is MANIFEST.PRN, and it will be placed on the directory you are using. You can specify a drive or directory and name by typing it into the place provided.

4 You can print the current selection of data, all of the data relating to a set of Topics, all of the general Overview data, or all of the Manifest information. The Tab key is used to switch selection between the boxes (Figure 4.12).

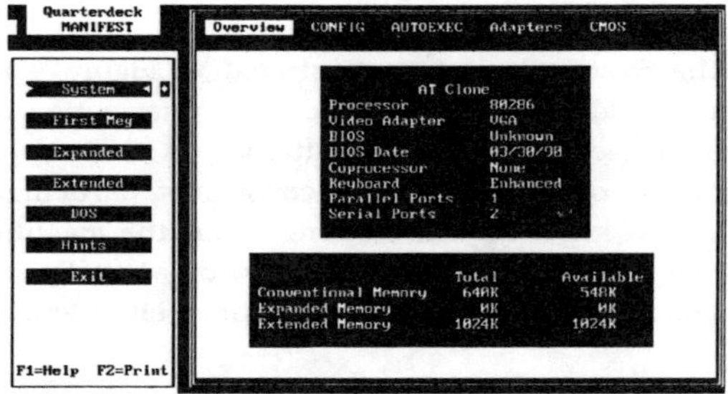

Figure 4.12 The Manifest menu with its topics selected from boxes along the top and down the left-hand side of the screen.

If you are doing anything other than making a check of what Manifest can do, it is useful to make a file of all of the Manifest information and to print this out later – a printed version is much more useful when you later want to make use of the information.

o Manifest, assuming it has been installed correctly, starts with a copyright notice, and then the System screen with a set of menus. The main menu is Overview.

The main areas in which Manifest can help are listed down the left-hand side for the Overview menu – these are System, First Meg, Expanded, Extended, DOS, DESQview, Hints and Exit. The DESQview option appears only if you are running Manifest from DESQview. If you are using a 386/486 machine with the QEMM-386 memory manager from DESQview this topic also will appear.

There is also a menu of options at the top of the screen to allow you to see information on the CON-FIG.SYS file, the AUTOEXEC.BAT file, the video system board, and the contents of CMOS memory.

o The Manifest report obtained from running it inside DESQview is different from the report that you get when running outside DESQview, because of the way that DESQview uses memory.

The illustrations here show Manifest running from MS-DOS.

The System report is illustrated in Figure 4.13 and provides much the same basic information as any of the other reporting utilities. It is a useful reminder of what the system consists of, particularly if you know next to nothing about the machine (some machines are supplied with virtually no documentation), and about its memory situation.

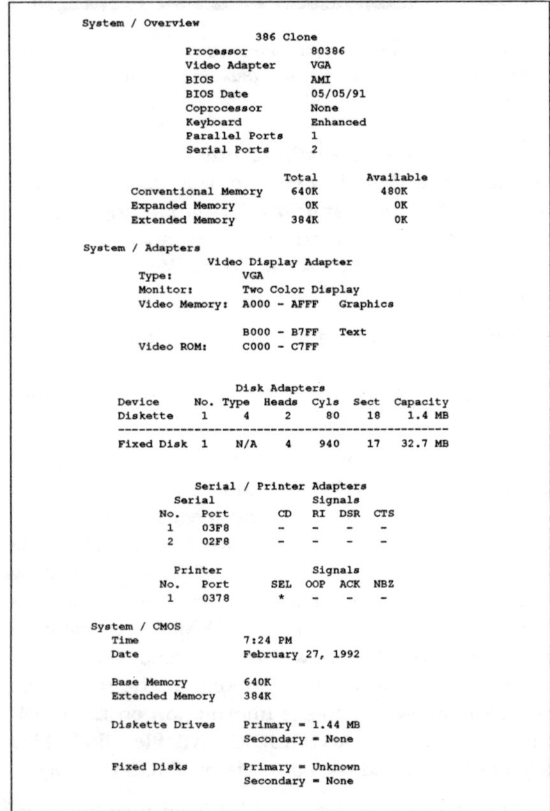

```
System / Overview
                        386 Clone
                Processor          80386
                Video Adapter      VGA
                BIOS               AMI
                BIOS Date          05/05/91
                Coprocessor        None
                Keyboard           Enhanced
                Parallel Ports     1
                Serial Ports       2

                                Total          Available
        Conventional Memory     640K             480K
        Expanded Memory          0K               0K
        Extended Memory         384K              0K

System / Adapters
                    Video Display Adapter
            Type:           VGA
            Monitor:        Two Color Display
            Video Memory:   A000 - AFFF   Graphics

                            B000 - B7FF   Text
            Video ROM:      C000 - C7FF

                        Disk Adapters
        Device      No. Type Heads  Cyls  Sect  Capacity
        Diskette     1    4    2      80    18    1.4 MB
        ---------------------------------------------------
        Fixed Disk   1   N/A   4     940    17   32.7 MB

                    Serial / Printer Adapters
                Serial              Signals
            No.    Port        CD   RI  DSR  CTS
             1     03F8        -    -   -    -
             2     02F8        -    -   -    -

                Printer             Signals
            No.    Port       SEL  OOP  ACK  NBZ
             1     0378        *    -   -    -

System / CMOS
    Time                    7:24 PM
    Date                    February 27, 1992

    Base Memory             640K
    Extended Memory         384K

    Diskette Drives         Primary = 1.44 MB
                            Secondary = None

    Fixed Disks             Primary = Unknown
                            Secondary = None
```

Figure 4.13 The Manifest System report for the machine shows useful information on the system memory and the memory used by the video card.

The reports on the First Meg menu are the most useful for analysing memory use. The example of Figure 4.14 shows the report for an unexpanded 386 machine, revealing (at the time) some 481 Kb of memory free.

```
First Meg / Overview
          Memory Area     Size    Description
          0000 - 003F       1K    Interrupt Area
          0040 - 004F     0.3K    BIOS Data Area
          0050 - 006F     0.5K    System Data
          0070 - 0F4D      59K    DOS
          0F4E - 27BE      97K    Program Area
          27BF - 9FFF     481K    [Available]
          ===Conventional memory ends at 640K===
          A000 - AFFF      64K    VGA Graphics
          B000 - B7FF      32K    VGA Text
          B800 - BFFF      32K    Unused
          C000 - C7FF      32K    Video ROM
          C800 - C9FF       8K    Disk ROM
          CA00 - EFFF     152K    Unused
          F000 - FFFF      64K    System ROM
```

Figure 4.14 The First Meg report of Manifest, covering this very important area of PC memory.

- Manifest shows addresses in hexadecimal, making it more difficult for you to use if you do not understand hex numbers. In addition, Manifest usually shows only the first four figures, the segment address, omitting a final zero.

- Manifest does not count the memory that it uses itself – this is included in the Available lot, but if you run Manifest from DESQview you will see the Available amount shrink because of the memory that is being used by DESQview.

The most interesting parts for the memory accounting are found beyond the 640 Kb limit. The illustration shows that there is 64 Kb used for video graphics, and if we wanted to work with a large text-based program this portion could be used. There are also two sections marked as Unused – one of 32 Kb and one of 152 Kb.

o These are *not* necessarily pieces of spare memory, however, only spare addresses.

On most PCs there are no RAM chips installed in the top 384 Kb part of the first 1 Mb of memory, except as part of a video board, so that though the address numbers are available for use, there is nothing to make use of them. This is a comparatively simple illustration that Manifest, like other memory reporting utilities, cannot work miracles – it can indicate how some memory address numbers are used, but it cannot necessarily tell if memory is present or if the reported use is likely to be true. You have to temper these reports with some common-sense, and be prepared to try things out.

o For example, a report may show 384 Kb of extended memory free, but on some chipsets part of it may have been used as Shadow RAM to copy data from the ROM.

Figure 4.15 shows the effect of using the Programs option of the First Meg set of reports. This shows that there are several short programs occupying the memory, the largest taking up 66 Kb and the smallest 0.3 Kb, with several programs using environment space where variables are temporarily stored. These programs are the resident programs which lurk in the memory until they are called – if SIDEKICK, for example, were installed on this particular machine this is where it would be found. As it happens, one of the programs shown here is for diverting printer output to a file, one is for the mouse, one is for controlling the keyboard, one provides a keyclick, and the remaining ones are part of the MS-DOS 5.0 files.

```
First Meg / Programs
        Memory Area     Size    Description
        0F4E - 1064     4.4K    COMMAND
        1065 - 1069     0.1K    [Available]
        106A - 107A     0.3K    COMMAND Environment
        107B - 1083     0.1K    KEYCLICK Environment
        1084 - 1084      0K     [Available]
        1085 - 1187      4K     DOSKEY
        1188 - 12B5     4.7K    KEYB
        12B6 - 12CB     0.3K    KEYCLICK
        12CC - 12D4     0.1K    PRN_FILE Environment
        12D5 - 167D     14K     MOUSE
        167E - 270E     66K     PRN_FILE
        270F - 2718     0.2K    COMMAND Data
        2719 - 27AD     2.3K    COMMAND
        27AE - 27BE     0.3K    COMMAND Environment
        27BF - 9FFF     481K    [Available]
```

Figure 4.15 Using the Programs option of the First Meg display.

- Each address number consists of the first four digits only (the segment address number), so that the address shown as 167E is really 167E0 (hexadecimal).

- These are all short programs and pieces of memory, but in all they amount to about 139 Kb and that is 139 Kb that cannot be used by anything else. If only some of the memory address above the 640 Kb limit were occupied by RAM, these programs could be shifted and would take up space that was less urgent.

Manifest is not a memory manager and cannot do that, but it can point to where there are spare address numbers and also to where there might be spare memory that memory manager programs can use, particularly on the 386 and 486 machines.

Several of the remaining reports concern interrupt numbers and other data of a more technical nature. This could be useful for an experienced programmer trying to solve problems of conflicts of accessories, but it is not vital to our search for more useful memory.

The Extended overview, however, is useful. The example (Figure 4.16) shows that there is extended memory in addresses from 1024 Kb to 1407 Kb, and that there is a memory manager (in this case, HIMEM.SYS from MS-DOS 5.0), making this memory available to any program that can use XMS (meaning, for most users, Windows 3.0 or 3.1).

```
Extended / Overview
        Memory Area      Size    Status
        1024K - 1407K    384K    Used from Top

Extended / XMS
        XMS Version              2.00
        Driver Revision          2.60
        High Memory Area         Available
        A20                      Disabled
        Handles Available        32
        Shares Memory with EMS   No

                                 Total      Largest
        Memory Block Type        Available  Available
        Upper (640K - 1024K)        0K         0K
        Extended (above 1024K)     320K       320K
```

Figure 4.16   Tracing the extended memory from the Extended Overview.

o The comment on the A20 line indicates that there is no program using extended memory at the instant of the report. The A20 line is the line of the address bus that deals with the second megabyte of RAM, and is normally disabled unless required (to ensure that there is no access to these memory areas other than through a memory manager program).

The final summary in this report shows that there is no Upper Memory (in the 640 Kb to 1 Mb region) and only 320 Kb of the 384 Kb of extended remaining (because MS-DOS is using 64 Kb of this memory), due to a DOS=HIGH line in the CONFIG.SYS file. Note that the A20 disabled report has not spotted the use of extended memory by HIMEM.SYS.

Memory managers

The use of one or more memory manager programs is essential if there is to be *any* use of memory above the 640 Kb barrier. The choice of memory managers is very wide and very confusing, because AT computers are usually supplied with some memory manager software, there are memory managers supplied with MS-DOS and DR-DOS, and there are memory managers supplied with expanded memory boards for XT machines.

o There is absolutely no guarantee that one memory manager will work alongside another from a different source, or that any memory manager will be able to prevent problems from appearing with certain programs on certain machines. It is better to assume that a memory manager will quite certainly conflict with any other from a different source.

This means that the selection of memory managers that need to work together has to be done with care, and the use of any memory manager involves some experiment and adjustment. At the simplest, this might only involve placing the memory manager command at the start of the CONFIG.SYS file rather than further down.

- It might, however, require you to use a complicated command line which excluded some memory addresses from being used.

- Windows 3.0 and 3.1 present a special case, because they contain their own memory management which will be invoked when you install Windows. This will be dealt with separately later.

The use of memory managers splits PC machines into three categories:

1 PC/XT machines for which a memory manager is useful only if a matching expanded memory board is fitted; remember that the cost of such a board could be put to better use in upgrading to an AT machine.

2 PC/AT 286 machines which can make limited use of a memory manager to use extended memory.

3 PC/AT 386 and 486 machines which can make full use of one or more memory managers to obtain some Upper memory (in the 640-1024 Kb region), control extended memory, and make use of extended memory as expanded memory for the benefit of programs that can use expanded memory.

At the time of writing, the falling prices of all machines make the 386 and 486 type of machine, whether in SX or DX form, the most attractive to users who are likely to need extra memory, so that they present the first priority.

o The following deals almost exclusively with the memory manager programs supplied by MS-DOS 5.0. This is because the majority of PC users will have these programs, but there are other memory manager programs, notably in DR-DOS 6.0 and as part of the DESQview suite of programs (from Quarterdeck UK), that are also very efficient for these purposes. Quarterdeck have been for a considerable time renowned for methods of squeezing the last drop of memory from PC machines.

Memory management – 386 machines

A 386 machine is very likely to be used with Windows, so that the comments on Windows memory management, later in this chapter, should be read. The following deals with memory management for purposes *other than Windows*, using the HIMEM.SYS and EMM386.SYS of MS-DOS 5.0, since these are the memory managers that virtually every owner of a 386 machine is likely to have by now. Users of DR-DOS 6.0 will have the corresponding EMM386.SYS program of DR-DOS installed.

MS-DOS 5.0 is provided with two memory managers. HIMEM.SYS is an extended memory manager which allows access to extended memory for DOS and for programs that use the XMS standard (at present, Windows and a very few others).

o Remember, however, that the heading of Windows includes any program that is designed to make use of Windows, and all of the leading software is either now available in this form or is being converted.

HIMEM.SYS also manages extended memory so as to avoid conflicts between programs, preventing programs from trying to make use of the same part of memory. HIMEM.SYS must be used before there is any attempt to make use of extended memory on any 80286, 80386 or 80486 machine.

This means that the first – or a very early – line of your CONFIG.SYS file should be:

```
DEVICE=HIMEM.SYS
```

assuming that the HIMEM.SYS file exists in the root directory of the hard disk.

● If HIMEM.SYS is, for example, in the MSDOS directory, the command should read:

```
DEVICE=C:\MSDOS\HIMEM.SYS
```

● A lot of trouble can be saved simply by ensuring that this is the first line of the CONFIG.SYS file, and checking that it is still the first line after installing new programs.

- There are still some programs about that modify CONFIG.SYS without notifying you and though it is unlikely that they would delete your own CONFIG.SYS they might substitute another with the HIMEM.SYS omitted, or with your own CONFIG.SYS instructions tacked on at the end.

The following CONFIG.SYS file shows HIMEM.SYS placed further down the list, but still in an acceptable position:

```
DEVICE=C:\MSDOS\SETVER.EXE
country=044
files= 30
buffers = 30
drivparm=/d:1 /f:2
DEVICE=C:\MSDOS\HIMEM.SYS
device=smartdrv.sys 310
SHELL=C:\MSDOS\COMMAND.COM C:\MSDOS\ /p
DOS=HIGH
```

In this case it is permissible because the first command that makes use of extended memory is the `device=smartdrv.sys` command.

- The CONFIG.SYS file, like the AUTOEXEC.BAT file, is one that varies from computer to computer, and you should not assume that commands shown in an example like this must necessarily appear on your own CONFIG.SYS file.

- If HIMEM.SYS is not placed first in the file it must certainly be placed ahead of any command that would make use of extended memory, such as, in this example, SMARTDRV.SYS or `DOS=HIGH`. Later versions of SMARTDrive can be run from either the CONFIG.SYS file or the AUTOEXEC.BAT file.

- HIMEM.SYS cannot be used along with version 2 of Windows, but this is in any case unlikely now that Windows 3 is fully established.

- HIMEM.SYS takes up a small amount of conventional memory, which must be balanced against the ability to release such memory by making use of extended memory.

- If you have used DOS=HIGH and get a message on booting up to the effect that DOS has been loaded in low memory, check to see if you have included HIMEM.SYS in the CONFIG.SYS file. If HIMEM.SYS is not present, DOS cannot be loaded into high (extended) memory. DOS will also load into low memory if there is any conflict caused by the first 64 Kb of extended memory being used for any other purposes.

HIMEM.SYS complications

The straightforward and simple HIMEM.SYS line illustrated above is as much as most users ever need. If problems arise that do not seem to arise from conflicts of memory-resident software (see later) it may be necessary to make use of some of the optional additions to the HIMEM command. Do not be discouraged by the long list of additions to the command, because these are designed for special circumstances, such as:

1 Fine tuning for faster use

2 Problems with older software

3 Problems with some hardware

The additions that follow can therefore be ignored unless complications arise, but before using any of these additions, check that HIMEM is correctly installed at or near the start of the CONFIG.SYS file, with the HIMEM.SYS program in the correct directory, and that problems are not caused by conflicts with other memory-resident programs.

Each addition or option to DEVICE=HIMEM.SYS is placed following a space and a slashmark, and more than one addition can be used (unless two would cancel each other).

1 Using DEVICE=HIMEM.SYS /HMAMIN=32 will reserve the extended memory for use by programs that need 32 Kb or more. This reserves extended

memory for programs that make more use of it. You can use figures from 0 to 63 in this option.

Without this addition, the first program requiring high memory will get exclusive use of all of it, even if it uses only a few bytes.

This is not as vital as it sounds because so few programs directly use extended memory. Ignore the addition unless a software manual specifically suggests that you use it.

2 Using `DEVICE=HIMEM.SYS /NUMHANDLES=64` will allocate 64 handles in place of the default 32. Numbers in the range 1 to 128 can be used.

A handle consists of six bytes of code in conventional memory that hold a description (for use by a program) of where part of the extended memory can be found. Handles are also used for locating expanded memory.

Programs that use extended memory will require at least one handle (for the program itself) and may need more (for data that the program uses).

The default setting of 32 is adequate for almost all likely eventualities, and this addition should be used only if a software manual (or a hint in a magazine) directs you to it.

3 Using `DEVICE=HIMEM.SYS /int15=64` is needed only by some old programs which use extended memory in a way that conflicts with HIMEM. The number allocates Kb of extended memory, and using a value less than 64 results in no allocation for these programs being made. Values of 64 to 65535 can be used, subject to sufficient memory being available.

Use this addition only if advised: it would be much better to upgrade any programs that required this addition.

4 Using `DEVICE=HIMEM.SYS /machine:1` specifies that the A20 handler is the correct one for the IBM PC/AT machine (or clone).

This ensures correct use of the A20 address line, unlocking the second megabyte of memory.

The A20 control is normally quite automatic, and this addition is needed only if A20 error messages are bring delivered. An example is:

```
Unable to control A20 line
```

It may also be necessary if the keyboard locks up when HIMEM is in use.

There are 14 codes which can be used following /machine: so as to correct the use of the A20 line for specific machines. If you are experiencing problems, check for your machine in the following list, but remember that code 1 is the default.

Code	Machine
1	IBM PC/AT or clone
2	IBM PC/2
3	Machine using Phoenix Cascade BIOS
4	HP Vectra A or A+
5	AT&T 6300+
6	Acer 110
7	Toshiba 1600 and 1200XE
8	Wyse 12.5 MHz 286
9	Tulip SX
10	Zenith ZBIOS
11	IBM PC/AT
12	CSS Labs
13	Philips; IBM PC/AT alternative delay
14	H-P vectra

A few machines use unexpected numbers, though most AT clones can use 1 as their A20 handler. The following additional list is known at the time of writing:

Machine	Number
Bull Micral 60	16
COMPUADD 386 systems	1 or 8
Datamedia 386/486	2
Hitachi HL500C	8
Intel 301z or 302	8
JDR 386/33	1
Toshiba 5100	7
UNISYS PowerPort	2

5 Using `DEVICE=HIMEM.SYS /A20CONTROL:ON` will force HIMEM to take control of the A20 address line whether it was on or off at the time when HIMEM took effect. This is the default. Using `/A20CONTROL:OFF` will allow HIMEM to take control of this line only if the line were OFF when HIMEM took effect.

In other words, using OFF allows other programs to take control of the A20 line even when HIMEM is to be used. This, once again, is rarely needed.

6 Using `DEVICE=CONFIG.SYS /SHADOWRAM:OFF` will switch off Shadow RAM on computers that can make use of this facility. Using `/SHADOWRAM:ON` will retain the shadow use. OFF is the default if the computer has 2 Mb or less of RAM.

Shadow RAM is extended RAM used by some chipsets, notably Chips & Technologies (C&T) and Headland. The ROM data is copied into this RAM and the machine is set to use this range of addresses rather than the ROM, because RAM is faster than ROM.

7 Using `DEVICE=CONFIG.SYS /CPUCLOCK:OFF` is a default setting, in which HIMEM is not allowed to change the clock speed (from Turbo to Slow). Using ON in place of OFF allows HIMEM to control the clock speed.

Using the ON setting will slow down the action of HIMEM.

Problems with HIMEM.SYS

Problems with HIMEM.SYS are almost all concerned with conflicts, particularly if another memory manager is present.

One common source of difficulty is a conflict with some memory-resident program that is loaded either in the CONFIG.SYS or AUTOEXEC.BAT files, and a useful way of checking is to keep copies of bare bones versions of these files, containing only the essential MS-DOS commands (such as KEYB,

DOS=HIGH and so on). If the problem disappears when these copies are used in place of the original then – by adding one program at a time, first to CONFIG.SYS and subsequently, if the problem does not re-appear, to AUTOEXEC.BAT – you should be able to trace the cause.

- Remember that it is also possible to remove a line in CONFIG.SYS or AUTOEXEC.BAT from use temporarily by starting it with REM. This does not work on elderly versions of MS-DOS, but is a useful way of making temporary checks on MS-DOS 5.0 and above.

- Remember also that you have to reboot to see any change in CONFIG.SYS take effect, and it is also desirable to reboot to see the new AUTOEXEC.BAT take effect, though you can type AUTOEXEC as a direct command.

- The Setup program for MS-DOS 5.0 will not even install HIMEM.SYS if another extended-memory manager program is active. If you have just upgraded to MS-DOS 5.0 and found that HIMEM.SYS is not present you will have to copy it by using EXPAND.EXE. Find the MS-DOS 5.0 disk which contains the file called HIMEM.SY_ and use EXPAND on this file to copy HIMEM.SYS to the hard disk.

- If you use the Intel Expanded-Memory Driver called EMM.SYS, you need to use the options /NE or /E when you install this driver with MS-DOS 5.0.

- If your computer uses a Phoenix BIOS and MS-DOS 5.0 HIMEM.SYS does not work correctly, add `/machine:1` or `/machine:8` to the `DEVICE=HIMEM.SYS` command in the CON-FIG.SYS file.

- If you use the XMAEM.SYS and XMA2EMS.SYS drivers, these are disabled when you use MS-DOS 5.0 SETUP. If both drivers were used together, you can obtain the same results by replacing them with `DEVICE=EMM386.EXE` (see later) in the CONFIG.SYS file. If you use the XMA card, remove the REM command that MS-DOS 5.0 puts into the CONFIG.SYS file ahead of the `DEVICE=XMA2EMS.SYS` command.

Using EMM386

HIMEM should be used (and will be automatically installed by MS-DOS 5.0) on any AT machine, whether 286, 386, 486 or higher. The other MS-DOS 5.0 memory manager utility, EMM386, is intended for use of 386 and 486 machines only; it cannot be run on 8088, 8086 or 80286 machines. Any attempt to run EMM386 on such machines will cause an error message.

EMM386 allows the extended memory of a 386 or 486 machine to be used for two distinct purposes:

1 To make use of RAM along with addresses in the Upper Memory Block (UMB), using the address region of 640 Kb to 1 Mb and taking RAM from part of the extended memory

2 To make use of extended memory (if it is available) as expanded memory for the programs that can use expanded memory, such as AutoSketch, DeLuxe Paint 2, etc.

The use of UMB memory is valuable, because several small programs can be loaded into that region and will run. Programs do not have to be specially written to be able to run in UMB memory, though there are a few which will not.

o By moving short memory-resident programs and utilities to UMB, conventional memory can be released, allowing large programs with no extended or expanded capabilities to make full use of the conventional memory.

EMM386 must not be used along with any other expanded memory managers. In other words, if your expanded memory is provided by a board in an expansion slot and needs to be managed by software provided with the board, do not install EMM386. Do not attempt to use EMM386 on a PC/XT machine or on an AT machine that uses the 80286 processor.

- Remember that you cannot use the same memory for two purposes. If you install EMM386 it will itself take around 80 Kb of extended memory, and the extended memory that it converts to UMB or expanded cannot be used also as extended memory.

- You can, however, use EMM386 for UMB uses only, leaving the rest of the extended memory free. This is well suited to machines with only 2 Mb of RAM.

- If you have 3 Mb or more of RAM, full use of EMM386 along with HIMEM can provide very flexible options for the programs that you are likely to run, other than Windows.

- Windows is always a special case, and EMM386 should not be used if you are intending to use only Windows programs. It can be installed if the programs you run under Windows are older programs which use expanded memory. For all other programs, Windows, aided by HIMEM.SYS, will manage memory for itself.

EMM386 is installed by a line in the CONFIG.SYS file that reads:

```
DEVICE=EMM386.EXE
```

This must follow the HIMEM line in the CONFIG.SYS file because EMM386 cannot take effect unless HIMEM is managing extended memory.

o There is another step that you need to take if you want to use the Upper Memory Blocks (see the next section).

EMM386 additions and switches

There are two additions that can be made to the EMM386 line in the CONFIG.SYS file.

1   Using `DEVICE=EMM386.EXE /NOEMS` will start up the EMM386 manager for Upper Memory Block management only, with no expanded memory supplied.

   This is useful if you have a small amount of extended RAM and you want to move short programs into UMB space to liberate the conventional memory.

2   Using `DEVICE=EMM386.EXE /RAM` will start up the EMM386 manager and allow it to control both UMB and expanded memory. This is the normal default, and should be used for machines with over 2 Mb of RAM. It must be used if you are running Lotus 1-2-3 V3.1, since this requires some expanded memory.

   If you want to use UMB memory for any purpose, you need to notify another part of the CONFIG.SYS file. You need either:

   (a)   To add `DOS=UMB` to the file

or:

   (b)   Change an existing `DOS=HIGH` to
   `DOS=HIGH,UMB`

This step connects the use of DOS in the conventional memory to its use in the UMB and is *essential* if you are to make any use of the UMB.

When this has been done, running `MEM /C` will give a readout such as that in Figure 4.17. This shows that SYSTEM is using 172032 bytes of the extended memory, consisting of parts of MS-DOS and parts of EMM386, and leaving 88 Kb free. This is a respectable amount which can be used for placing programs into UMB, a topic dealt with in Chapter 5.

Note that there is 8.2 Kb of conventional memory also used by EMM386.

```
Conventional Memory :

   Name                  Size in Decimal          Size in Hex
--------------          -----------------------   --------------
   MSDOS                 12304     ( 12.0K)          3010
   SETVER                  400     (  0.4K)           190
   HIMEM                  2896     (  2.8K)           B50
   EMM386                 8400     (  8.2K)          20D0
   COMMAND                2624     (  2.6K)           A40
   KEYCLICK                432     (  0.4K)           1B0
   DOSKEY                 4128     (  4.0K)          1020
   KEYB                   5360     (  5.2K)          14F0
   MOUSE                 16976     ( 16.6K)          4250
   FREE                     64     (  0.1K)            40
   FREE                     96     (  0.1K)            60
   FREE                 601376     (587.3K)         92D20

Total  FREE :           601536     (587.4K)

Upper Memory :

   Name                  Size in Decimal          Size in Hex
--------------          -----------------------   --------------
   SYSTEM               172032     (168.0K)         2A000
   FREE                  90080     ( 88.0K)         15FE0

Total  FREE :            90080     ( 88.0K)

Total bytes available to programs (Conventional+Upper) :     691616    (675.4K)
Largest executable program size :                            601376    (587.3K)
Largest available upper memory block :                        90080    ( 88.0K)

     393216 bytes total contiguous extended memory
          0 bytes available contiguous extended memory
     150528 bytes available XMS memory
            MS-DOS resident in High Memory Area
```

*Figure 4.17 The MEM report that shows UMB memory
activated by EMM386.*

Using EMM386 for expanded memory

When the DEVICE=EMM386.EXE line, with or without
the /RAM addition, is used, EMM386 is activated for
both expanded memory and for UMB use, though
the UMB use is more limited because of the address
range used for expanded memory.

Figure 4.18 is a MEM /C report which shows that
the use of EMM386 has resulted in 24 Kb of UMB
becoming available on a machine with 1 Mb of total
RAM. There is also some 196608 bytes of expanded
(EMS) memory free, and 8192 bytes of extended
memory remaining because EMM386 has not taken
this last portion.

```
Conventional Memory :

   Name                 Size in Decimal        Size in Hex
---------------      --------------------    ---------------
   MSDOS                 12304   ( 12.0K)        3010
   SETVER                  400   (  0.4K)         190
   HIMEM                  2896   (  2.8K)         B50
   EMM386                 8400   (  8.2K)        20D0
   COMMAND                2624   (  2.6K)         A40
   KEYCLICK                432   (  0.4K)         1B0
   DOSKEY                 4128   (  4.0K)        1020
   KEYB                   5360   (  5.2K)        14F0
   MOUSE                 16976   ( 16.6K)        4250
   FREE                     64   (  0.1K)          40
   FREE                     96   (  0.1K)          60
   FREE                 601376   (587.3K)       92D20

Total  FREE :          601536   (587.4K)

Upper Memory :

   Name                 Size in Decimal        Size in Hex
---------------      --------------------    ---------------
   SYSTEM               172032   (168.0K)       2A000
   FREE                  24544   ( 24.0K)        5FE0

Total  FREE :           24544   ( 24.0K)

Total bytes available to programs (Conventional+Upper) :   626080   (611.4K)
Largest executable program size :                          601376   (587.3K)
Largest available upper memory block :                      24544   ( 24.0K)

    589824 bytes total EMS memory
    196608 bytes free EMS memory

    393216 bytes total contiguous extended memory
         0 bytes available contiguous extended memory
      8192 bytes available XMS memory
           MS-DOS resident in High Memory Area
```

Figure 4.18 A MEM /C report showing EMM386 being used to provide both UMB and expanded memory on a machine with only 1 Mb free RAM.

o The reference to Total EMS Memory means how much EMS memory can be addressed; it does not mean that such memory exists, unless there are memory chips installed for at least 2 Mb total. The Free EMS figure shows what is actually present and available for use.

An important point in this report is that there is now some 611 Kb that can be used by programs. Of this, most is in the conventional part of the memory below the 640 Kb mark, and a little is in the UMB. By shifting programs to UMB, even if only MOUSE.COM, a substantial gain will be made for conventional memory.

EMM386 complications

For most users, the default values that EMM386 uses are sufficient, and the only decision that needs to be made is whether or not to use the /NOEMS option. The options and additions that can be used with EMM386 are useful only if they are required and if you know how to use them.

- What this boils down to is that you should use such options only where there is a conflict of memory and you are advised to change the EMM386 command.

- Experimenting with these options and additions can cause your computer to lock up and you will be unable to restart it unless you have a floppy formatted as a system disk, with a CONFIG.SYS and AUTOEXEC.BAT that contain no commands that might be problematic.

- It is useful to have, as noted for HIMEM.SYS, at least two system floppy disks with no CON-FIG.SYS or AUTOEXEC.BAT (or with minimal files that are known to cause no problems), so as to ensure that nothing is loaded into RAM.

The following list of EMM386 options, therefore, is for information only and can be used to cross-check advice that you may have received in the event of a lock-up occurring.

o Remember that the use of high memory is always slightly problematic because of the interaction of different programs. Before you consider any alterations to the EMM386 command, try booting with memory-resident programs removed from the AUTOEXEC.BAT file. This can be done by placing the word REM ahead of each command line which is to be ignored.

1 Using DEVICE=EMM386 /W=ON will enable the use of a Weitek maths co-processor. This is unusual, and most users of co-processors specify the simpler units made by INTEL, IIT or CYRIX. A Weitek processor is likely to cost more than the

rest of a small computer. The ON can be changed to OFF if necessary, but this is the default if the /W option is not used.

2 Using `DEVICE=EMM368 /M:1` specifies that the expanded memory page frame will start at the address C000 (hexadecimal). The *page frame* is the start of the address for a 64 Kb piece of expanded memory; the actual address corresponding to C000 is C0000 hexadecimal, 768 Kb.

This is useful only if you need to force the start of the page frame to one of a preset range of addresses. This starting address is normally located automatically.

The address numbers that correspond to the code numbers, along with the equivalent number of kilobytes from the start of memory, in this command are as follows:

Code	Address (hex)	Kilobytes equivalent
1	C0000	768
2	C4000	784
3	C8000	800
4	CC000	816
5	D0000	832
6	D4000	848
7	D8000	864
8	DC000	880
9	E0000	896
10	80000	512
11	84000	528
12	88000	544
13	8C000	560
14	90000	576

Numbers 10 to 14 inclusive are used only for a machine in which the last 128 Kb has been disabled, so that it has only 512 Kb of conventional RAM.

3 `DEVICE=EMM368 /FRAME=D400` would have the effect of forcing a page frame to start at the

address D4000 (hex). Only the range of hex numbers shown above can be used.

4 `DEVICE=EMM368 /PD000` would make the frame start at D0000: another way of specifying the starting address.

These alternatives are used so as to be compatible with other expanded memory drivers.

5 `DEVICE=EMM368 /P1=D400` makes page 1 of expanded memory use D4000 hex as its starting address.

The starting addresses for pages 0 to 3 inclusive must follow on from each other.

6 `DEVICE=EMM368 /x=C000 D000` prevents EMM386 from using this specified range of addresses (taken from the list above).

This can be used if a range of addresses must not be used but for some reason; it is not detected when EMM386 is started. If you use an XGA display with EMM386.EXE, you may need to use this command to exclude some memory ranges. To decide which memory ranges to exclude you will need to look at the memory map when the XGA display is in use.

7 `DEVICE=EMM368 /i=D000 E000` specifies that this range of addresses, corresponding to D0000 to E0000, can be used for expanded memory use.

8 `DEVICE=EMM368 /B=2000` specifies that the address 20000 (hexadecimal) is the lowest that will be used for swapping 16 Kb sets of data during the use of expanded memory. The default number is 4000 (address 40000).

It would be very unusual to need to change this.

9 `DEVICE=EMM368 /L=500` specifies that 500 Kb of extended memory should be left over after EMM386 has created expanded memory. The default is zero.

This could be useful if you need a mixture of expanded and extended memory and have enough RAM installed to cater for both.

10 `DEVICE=EMM368 /A=10` specifies that storage space for ten alternate registers will be used. This storage is used to preserve the state of a program that has been frozen while another program is running. The default is 7, allowing seven programs to be running at one time.

Normally, you would carry out this multi-tasking type of action only by way of Windows, which attends to the memory management automatically.

11 `DEVICE=EMM368 /H=32` specifies that 32 handles will be allocated for controlling files. The default is 64.

This should not be altered unless you have a good reason for needing to change it.

12 `DEVICE=EMM368 /D=32` keeps 32 Kb free for a buffer to manage *direct memory access* (DMA) actions, other than those for floppy disks. The default is 16 and it is most unlikely that you would need to alter the amount.

The EMM386 direct command

In addition to the use of EMM386 as an installed memory manager, MS-DOS provides the EMM386 command as a way of checking and modifying the action of the manager. Typing EMM386 will produce a report such as that in Figure 4.19. The useful part of this shows that, in this example, 192 Kb of EMS expanded memory is now available.

```
MICROSOFT Expanded Memory Manager 386  Version 4.20.06X
(C) Copyright Microsoft Corporation 1986, 1990

  Available expanded memory . . . . . . . .    192 KB

  LIM/EMS version . . . . . . . . . . . . .    4.0
  Total expanded memory pages . . . . . . .     36
  Available expanded memory pages . . . . .     12
  Total handles . . . . . . . . . . . . . .     64
  Active handles  . . . . . . . . . . . . .      1
  Page frame segment  . . . . . . . . . . .  D000 H

  Total upper memory available  . . . . . .      0 KB
  Largest Upper Memory Block available  . .      0 KB
  Upper memory starting address . . . . . .  CA00 H

EMM386 Active.
```

Figure 4.19 The report obtained by using EMM386 as a command.

o Using the EMM386 command like this produces a report that states that no Upper Memory Blocks are available. This contradicts the MEM report on the same setup which shows 24 Kb available in UMB for the same setup.

The EMM386 command can be followed by options that enable it, disable it, or allow EMM386 to come into action when required. For example, using EMM368 /ON will force EMM386 on and EMM386 /OFF will force it off. Using EMM386 /AUTO will allow EMM386 to be used when required.

o This allows you to disable and re-enable EMM386 in the course of working with programs.

You can also use /W=ON to enable the use of a Weitek co-processor (see earlier) or /W=OFF to disable the action.

Using a 286 computer

The options provided for a 286 computer using MS-DOS utilities are usually much more limited compared to the 386 or 486 type of machine, unless you are fortunate enough to have a machine that uses a suitable chipset with Shadow RAM or the ability to use extended memory as expanded memory (see later).

● You cannot use EMM386.EXE on a 286 machine, and any attempt to do so will be met with a message that EMM386 has not been installed.

● The 286 processor simply cannot deal with extended memory in the same way as the 386 or 486, which is why machines based on this chip, though fast and useful, are considered obsolescent.

You can use HIMEM.SYS with the 286 chip to manage the extended memory up to a maximum of 16 Mb (total RAM). MS-DOS 5.0 will use part of the extended memory to run some of the MS-DOS system, freeing up conventional memory.

- You cannot, however, run programs in the extended memory other than by using Windows.

- You cannot convert part of the extended memory into expanded by using EMM386. This is because the 80286 (and higher) chips can address extended memory only by switching into a mode that makes it impossible to run MS-DOS. On the 80286, no provision was made for easily switching back from this mode, a fundamental design flaw in this chip. There are, however, some utilities that can make use of extended memory as if it were expanded.

You can use the extended memory to run a cache or RAMdrive (see Chapter 5), and you can, if you wish, install an expanded memory board, along with an expanded memory driver (not from MS-DOS) to carry out some of the actions of EMM386.

Though these options look restricted, the additional conventional memory space that is released by placing MS-DOS into high memory allows a 286 machine to run virtually all of the programs that the 386 machine can run, though sacrificing some features (such as easy use of expanded memory). The design of the 286 chip (see above) makes it virtually impossible to use extended memory as if it were expanded memory.

- The well-planned use of cache and RAMdrive can make a 286 machine very fast, and it can run Windows well if it has enough extended memory.

- The use of an expanded memory board with a 286 machine makes it possible to relocate some programs into this memory, using memory managers such as QRAM from Quarterdeck (see Appendix B). In addition, there are Quarterdeck utilities packed with QRAM that allow the use of some video memory if this is available. The expanded memory can be used for expansion with extended memory being used for cache or RAMdrive.

There are exceptions for some types of machines with chipsets that either provide RAM or can control extended memory. The Chip & Technologies set uses Shadow RAM, meaning RAM that is mapped to the same addresses as ROM and with the ROM contents copied into RAM when the machine is booted. Since RAM is faster than ROM, this appreciably speeds up the action of the machine.

o More important for memory use, the Shadow RAM can be commandeered by some memory management utilities, notable these from Quarterdeck. Considerable care is needed to ensure that the machine does not try to use this RAM for both purposes.

Machines that use the Headland chipset can also, in some cases, make use of extended memory as expanded memory if the Headland G2 GC103 memory controller is used. This requires the EMS option to be selected in the CMOS SETUP and a driver called MM.SYS to be placed in the CONFIG.SYS file and configured to provide the expanded memory amount that is needed to allow UMB use.

● This is not a simple task, and though the MM.SYS software may be supplied with the computer there is no certainty that it will work with the chipset that exists on the board, or that you will be able to use any extended memory.

● Several machines provide for management of extended memory from the CMOS SETUP menu. You are often able to determine how much of the extended memory can be used as Shadow RAM, as EMS expanded memory and as ordinary extended memory. You still need HIMEM.SYS to control the use of the remaining extended memory, and you need to remember that there will be conflicts if your software tries to use the memory differently.

XT machines

The old XT machine using the 8088 or 8086 chip comes at the bottom of the heap as far as memory management is concerned. The only possibility of expansion and more efficient memory use is by way of expanded memory boards, using the expanded memory driver software for whichever type of board is used.

- If expanded memory exists, the QRAM set of utilities from Quarterdeck can make maximum use of it, allowing you to place memory-resident programs into part of the expanded memory.

- For a straightforward PC with 640 Kb of conventional memory and no expanded memory, but using a VGA (or EGA) screen display, QRAM can provide an extra 96 Kb for a program that makes no use of graphics.

Using WINDOWS

At the time of writing, Windows 2 is obsolete, and users of Windows should have upgraded to versions 3.0 or (preferably) 3.1.

o These later versions are not intended for PC/XT machines using the 8088 or 8086 chips, so that the Windows 3 software contains extended memory manager features for both 286 and 386 machines.

It is important to note that Windows is by no means essential to your use of a PC computer. If your interest is in running one program on one machine for most of each day, the use of Windows is little more than an expensive way of slowing down the action of the machine, and if memory is needed, the use of HIMEM and EMM386 will provide it without the need to use Windows. Programs other than the specially-written (and expensive) Windows programs can be run much faster without

Windows, and with a considerable saving in memory.

Windows becomes useful if the type of computing you do requires you to change from one program to another at frequent intervals, but without closing down the programs. For this type of application, Windows saves the time that would normally be spent in saving data, closing down a program, opening another one and reading in data. You might, however, find that you can be more productive by using two machines rather than by time-sharing one, which is what Windows can do.

- Windows allows you to switch from one running program to another, either keeping the previous program in the background, or reducing it to a reminder, an icon at the foot of the screen.

- In addition, it is possible (particularly on 386 machines) to leave a program running in the background, so that a spreadsheet could be engaged in a long calculation while you worked with a word processor on the main part of the screen.

- For details of the workings of Windows, see the *Windows 3 Pocket Book* from Heinemann New-tech.

Windows 3 makes use of extended memory, and will work co-operatively with SMARTDrive, so that the cache will reduce in size when Windows needs more memory and increase again when Windows does not require additional memory.

The provision of large amounts of extended memory is very important for Windows, because when a program is *swapped out* – put into the background so that another program can be run – the swapped out program can be placed in extended memory.

- Swapping to memory is fast. If insufficient extended memory is available, all such swapping will be to disk, which is very much slower. In addition, when Windows runs in its standard mode (on a 286, or on a 386 with less than 2 Mb RAM) it will, by default, use the hard disk for swapping non-Windows programs.

- Ideally, Windows 3 should be used with a fast 386 machine and at least 4 Mb of memory. Anything less is likely to be slow on actions that require a lot of program swapping.

Windows 3.0 did not fully manage to avoid conflicts of memory. A memory conflict was usually signalled by an Unrecoverable Application Error (UAE) message (not mentioned in the manual). This suspended all actions and pressing the Enter key would then allow you to escape back to MS-DOS, with all Windows data lost. These conflicts often had unexpected causes, such as Super VGA driver software used in conjunction with programs which were otherwise well behaved.

Windows 3.1 has been greatly improved in this respect, but it is important to make full use of the suite of mouse and video drivers and other software that comes with Windows, rather than using corresponding software from other sources.

- There are even conflicts between Windows 3.0 and MS-DOS 5.0 when a 386 machine is used with 2 Mb or less of memory and EMM386 is in use. There is little point in using EMM386 along with Windows when you use only Windows programs, but HIMEM.SYS is essential.

- EMM386 can be used to provide expanded memory for programs that require it if you want to run such programs under Windows. If you are using a 386 machine with more than 2 Mb of RAM, add the /D=48 option to the EMM386 command. It is usually better and much faster to run such programs without using Windows.

Users of Windows 3.0 who experience memory shortages using Program Manager can gain memory by replacing PROGMAN.EXE by MSDOS.EXE. This is done as follows:

1 Using Windows Notepad, look at the file called SYSTEM.INI.

2 Find the line (usually the first line) `SHELL=PROGMAN.EXE`.

3 Alter this to `SHELL=MSDOS.EXE`.

4 This makes the main display one of named files rather than icons, using very much less memory.

o Windows 3.1 Program Manager is very much more efficient and uses much less memory. There is no need to replace it.

Avoiding conflicts

The following points concern some of the better known problems that can arise with Windows 3.0 and 3.1. Note that there are differences between Windows 3.0 and 3.1, particularly concerning the use of EMM386.EXE.

1 If you use the UMB region to hold device drivers and other memory-resident programs, and you also run DOS (non-Windows) programs that use expanded memory, modify the `DEVICE=EMM386.EXE` command in the CONFIG.SYS file to read:

```
DEVICE=EMM386.EXE /RAM
```

2 If you start Windows in 386 enhanced mode and get a message stating:

```
EMM386: Unable to start Enhanced Mode
Windows due to invalid path
specification for EMM386
```

the cause is that EMM386.EXE is not in the root directory. Either move it to the root, or alter the EMM386 line so as to read:

```
DEVICE=EMM386.EXE /Y=C:\MSDOS\EMM386.EXE
```

(Assuming in this example that the EMM386.EXE file is in the \MSDOS directory.)

Remember that if your use of EMM386.EXE takes up too much memory, Windows will always start in standard, not enhanced, mode. Do not use EMM386 to create expanded memory unless you have adequate RAM memory or it is essential to the programs you are running. Alternatively, consider using standard instead of enhanced mode.

3 Shifting the WINA20.386 file. When a 386 machine has adequate RAM, Windows will start in 386 Enhanced mode, and Windows Setup will install a read-only file named WINA20.386 in the root directory of the hard disk. If this file is moved to a different directory you need to make two changes:

> **(a)** Add to the CONFIG.SYS file the line:
>
> ```
> SWITCHES=/W
> ```
>
> **(b)** Add to the [386Enh] section of the SYSTEM.INI file (in the Windows directory) a line that shows the path to WINA20.386, such as:
>
> ```
> DEVICE=C:\WINDOWS\WINA20.386
> ```
>
> (Assuming in this example that WINA20.386 has been shifted to the WINDOWS directory.)

4 If you use the `DEVICE=EMM386.EXE` command in the CONFIG.SYS file, you cannot run Windows 3.0 in standard mode. You must either remove the `DEVICE=EMM386.EXE` command or run Windows in real or enhanced mode. Windows 3.1 runs only in standard or enhanced modes.

Remember that using EMM386 will take up extended memory, leaving Windows with less.

5 Windows 3.1 Setup carries out a check for memory-resident programs and will report on any that are known to cause problems. This allows you to abort the Setup and remove the offending programs. The program that you are most likely to have that will cause such a report is FASTOPEN.

5 Speed and Memory Use

Using UMB memory – 386 machines

The 80386, 80486 and other microprocessor chips of this family that are planned for future use have an internal organisation that is very much better than that of the 80286, and one of the many advantages is that some extended memory can be allocated to addresses in the Upper Memory region: addresses between the 640 Kb barrier and the 1 Mb mark. All of these are addresses that MS-DOS 5.0 can use provided the essential UMB command is placed in the line (see Chapter 4) in the CONFIG.SYS file. This will normally make such a line read:

```
DOS=HIGH,UMB
```

since you will normally want to place part of MS-DOS into the Upper Memory Block regions.

o The use of UMB is very similar to that of expanded memory, and the same EMM386 manager deals with both. If you want to use UMB only and not expanded memory, make sure that your EMM386 line specifies this (see Chapter 4).

The difference between expanded memory and UMB (Figure 5.1) is that UMB is extended memory that is permanently assigned to addresses in the UMB region, not swapped around in 64 Kb pieces. This makes the use of UMB faster, though the amount of UMB is restricted to the number of free addresses. For example, you can use 64 Kb of UMB if you have 64 Kb of spare addresses, but this number of free addresses could allow the use of several megabytes of expanded memory in 64 Kb pieces.

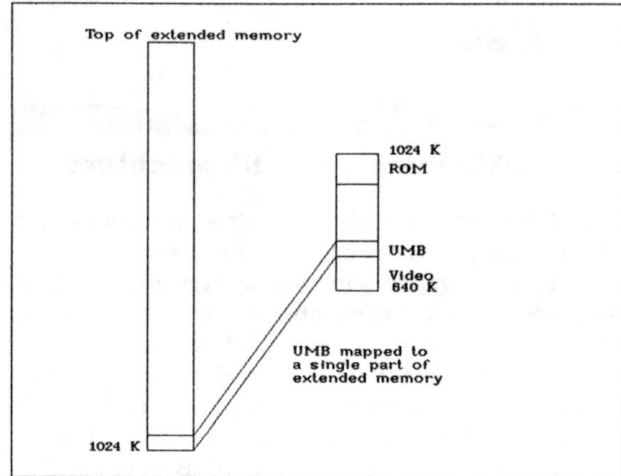

Figure 5.1   The essential difference between UMB memory and expanded memory is that a UMB address accesses a fixed portion of extended memory; an EMS address can access several parts of extended memory, one at a time.

The UMB is generally used to clear conventional memory of as many memory-resident utilities as possible. There would be little point in using UMB for ordinary programs which take up memory only while in use, but for any program that requires to hold on to memory all the time the computer is running, the use of UMB is a splendid way of releasing conventional memory. Programs such as MOUSE.COM, SMARTDRV.EXE, KEYB and so on are obvious candidates for UMB residence, because otherwise they take up a considerable amount of space in conventional memory.

o The commands for making use of UMB are therefore mainly placed in the CONFIG.SYS and AUTOEXEC.BAT files. The commands that are used to place program files into UMB memory are slightly different from the commands used for normal installation.

Placing programs in UMB

In the CONFIG.SYS file, the main use for UMB will be to hold drivers, meaning lines that start 'DEVICE=' and specify a program to place into memory. When such a driver is to be placed into UMB memory, the command will start as 'DEVICEHIGH=' and continue as before.

You cannot put all DEVICE lines into UMB memory, and in particular you must ensure that UMB memory has been activated before you attempt to place any drivers into it.

1 Make sure that the lines:

```
DEVICE=HIMEM.SYS
DEVICE=EMM386.SYS
DOS=HIGH.UMB
```

are all placed ahead of the drivers you want to put into UMB.

2 Add the DEVICEHIGH lines you need, such as.

```
DEVICEHIGH=RAMDRIVE.SYS 512 /E
```

3 Reboot and check that the memory is being correctly allocated and used.

Most of the memory-eating resident programs are loaded from the AUTOEXEC.BAT file, and the command LOADHIGH is used to force these programs to run in the UMB.

1 Inspect your AUTOEXEC.BAT file to see what parts might be loaded high. A typical file might appear as:

```
@ECHO OFF
PATH C:\;C:\MSDOS
set dircmd=/w/p/o:gn
set temp=c:\temp
C:\MSDOS\doskey /insert > nul
keyb uk,,C:\keyboard.sys
setvid vga
keyclick
mouse
```

2 In such a list, the main memory-resident parts are DOSKEY, KEYB, KEYCLICK and MOUSE.

3 Use MEM to show the size of each of these programs and grade them in order of size, largest first. Re-arrange the lines of your AUTOEXEC.BAT file so that the lines are in this descending order of size.

4 Use a LOADHIGH in each line, ahead of the main command portion, thus:

```
@ECHO OFF
PATH C:\;C:\MSDOS
set dircmd=/w/p/o:gn
set temp=c:\temp
setvid vga
loadhigh mouse
loadhigh keyb uk,,C:\keyboard.sys
loadhigh C:\MSDOS\doskey /insert > nul
loadhigh keyclick
```

This revised file will load in the programs using UMB. The point of loading the programs in descending order of size is to allow as many of them as possible to be squeezed in. If a set of small programs is loaded they will often take more memory than they need, and it is always more important to be able to place the larger programs into UMB.

- If there is not enough UMB space, the last program(s) will remain in conventional memory. It is better that these are short programs than long ones.

- On a few machines there may be difficulty with loading device drivers or programs into the upper memory area, caused by the way that the hard disk management system works. In such cases, adding a `DEVICE=SMARTDRV.SYS` command (or its equivalent) before any DEVICEHIGH commands in the CONFIG.SYS file is often useful. If you use SMARTDRV.EXE, place it into the CONFIG.SYS file by using:

```
INSTALL=SMARTDRV.EXE
```

Speed of machine

Machines themselves can be fast or slow, and two factors that contribute considerably are the type of processor and the clock speed that it uses. The older processors such as the 8088 and 8086 are very much slower than the later 80286, 80386 and 80486. As a rough guide, the 80286 is, under similar working conditions, some six times faster than the 8088.

o The 80386 processor is faster than the 80286, and the 80486 is faster than the 80386.

In addition, the speed at which a processor can work is determined to a considerable extent by its *clock rate*. This is the rate, in terms of pulses per second, that electrical controlling pulses are delivered to the microprocessor chip from a circuit called the *clock*.

o The rate of the clock is measured in units called *megahertz*, abbreviated to MHz, and meaning million pulses per second.

The timing of every action in a computer is determined by these clock pulses, though only a few chips use the clock pulses at their full speed; other parts of the machine use a sub-multiple such as one pulse in four, one in six and so on.

o Early 8088 machines used a 4.77 MHz clock which is now considered to be very slow; recent 80386 machines have used clock speeds as high as 50 MHz. Later 8086 XT machines have used 8 MHz clock speeds and the most common speed for the 80386 is 25 MHz.

Though clock speed is a good indicator of machine speed, it has to be regarded with some caution if applied to different processors, because the 80486, for example, running at 25 MHz, is still faster than the 80386 running at 33 MHz.

o In addition, the clock rate indicates only how fast the microprocessor itself can run. It does not imply that the rest of the system will be fast.

A microprocessor working at a high clock rate may be spending a considerable amount of its time idling, waiting for data from other chips, from the keyboard or from the hard disk. In addition, the memory chips may not be fast enough to keep up with the processor.

- When memory is too slow, machines sometimes use *wait states*, meaning that the microprocessor will do nothing for several clock pulses while it is accessing memory. This gives the memory time to read or write data.

- The worst bottleneck in a system usually occurs when a program has to make use of a large number of disk read and write actions, because anything that requires mechanical actions such as moving a disk head is inevitably much slower than purely electrical actions such as using memory.

Conflicting requirements

There is a fundamental conflict between speed and the requirement for larger and larger amounts of memory. A really fast program would be one that used less than 64 Kb of RAM and was written so as to make maximum use of the fastest commands of the microprocessor. These were the programs that were written in the early days of the PC machine (when machine clock speeds were slow), and very few programs written nowadays are of this type.

o In general, programs with a COM extension will load faster and run faster than programs with the EXE extension.

In the early days of the PC, programs were often written directly in 'machine code', which ensured that they were very compact and fast running. This way of writing programs is, however, fiendishly difficult for larger programs, and not adaptable to use by teams of programmers. Modern programs, other than some shareware programs, are usually written in a high-level language, meaning that instructions are written and translated into machine code by a program called a *compiler.*

o The compiler does not generate such compact and fast-running code as writing machine code directly, so that programs created by this method are inevitably larger and slower.

Nevertheless, when programs are run from MS-DOS directly, by typing the name of the program and pressing the Enter key, they will run faster than is ever possible when some form of *shell* program is being used.

● A shell program is one that tries to avoid the direct use of MS-DOS commands and reduces the need for typing. Typically, a shell program allows you to run programs by selecting a program name or icon with the mouse and clicking the mouse button.

● All shells take up memory which otherwise could be used by your program, and because they are an intermediate between you and the MS-DOS operating system they also add time.

● No form of shell *replaces* MS-DOS; it simply acts as a form of interpreter between you, the user, and the MS-DOS commands. Only a totally new operating system, such as NT, will avoid the time wasted in using an intermediate shell.

Some shell programs can make use of the text screen, like MS-DOS DOSSHELL, DR-DOS VIEW-MAX or Quarterdeck DESQview. These programs are reasonably fast running, because the text screen of the PC responds faster than the graphics screen (which has more bytes to control). Furthermore, when a program is loaded and run, the shell is removed, except for a small kernel, so that the shell does not take up any more memory than is essential.

o This allows large programs to be loaded and run without seriously depleting the memory, even if only 640 Kb is available with no extended or expanded memory.

The other option is to use a shell that employs the graphics screen. This is slower and requires more of the video memory to be used. Windows is the best known modern example of the graphics type of shell program, though DR GEM was used on some machines (notably the older Amstrads) and with some well known software (such as the early versions of Ventura Publisher).

o Windows contains its own memory management for extended memory, and the most recent 3.0 and 3.1 versions are not intended to be used by machines such as PC/XT machines that cannot use extended memory and which have not been fitted with expanded memory boards.

Using a cache

Since the most constricting influence on speed is disk access, the use of a disk cache is by far the best way of increasing the speed of any AT machine.

A disk cache uses some memory, usually extended memory, to hold information which is read from the disk or is to be written to the disk.

o If data is being read frequently, a cache can hold enough data to ensure that the data can usually be supplied from the cache rather than directly from the disk.

For frequent writes, the cache can hold data until there is too much to hold in memory and a disk write is essential. In either case, the cache is the main reservoir of data, and the computer reads from and writes to the cache if possible.

o Since the cache is memory, this reading and writing can be fast and efficient.

If the cache is being used for writing and the cache fills up, the content of the cache is saved to the disk. If the cache is being used for reading, the first request for data will cause the hard disk to be read and to read enough to fill the cache. Subsequent reads will be from the cache unless the data required is not in the cache, which will cause the disk to be read again.

o A small cache for reading is not efficient if small amounts of data are read from scattered parts of the disk, but if the cache is large it may hold almost all the contents of a disk.

If extended memory is used for a cache, a large amount of memory can be devoted to the cache, typically 1 Mb. A cache of this size will hold most of the contents of a 1.2 Mb or 1.4 Mb disk and can greatly speed up disk actions. The use of extended memory as cache requires software to manage the use of the memory, a point dealt with in Chapter 4.

A disk cache can be read only or read/write. Using a read-only cache is safe, because all the data that is being cached is duplicated on the disk, and if anything should happen to cause a reboot (a hiccup in the power line, for example) no data will be lost.

o A read/write cache, by contrast, carries the risk that there will be some data in the cache that has not been written to the disk, though as far as the program you are using is concerned, it has been saved. A reboot that is carried out for any reason will result in this data being lost.

Cache programs with cache writing as well as reading usually try to get around this hazard by writing data to the hard disk whenever there is a period in which the disk is not being used, and they also provide for a write command which can be used to force a write if you want to reboot and are not certain that the cache has written data.

● It is possible to write a short batch file that will ensure that the cache is written and then reboot the machine, and this batch file can be called instead of simply pressing Ctrl-Alt-Del.

● If you are using a read/write cache and you run programs from batch files, the write-to-disk command can be the last command in the batch file, making the action automatic.

Neither of these safeguards, however, will prevent data from being lost if you switch off abruptly or suffer a power cut, and if data is very precious it is probable better to disable write caching. SMARTDrive and other cache programs allow this to be done by using an option letter in the command that starts the cache running.

- SMARTDrive from Microsoft is one well-known cache memory manager of this kind and, of the versions available at the time of writing, the best and most recent is packaged along with Windows 3.1. This is version 4.0.091, a file called SMARTDRV.EXE, and it is, unlike the older SMARTDRV.SYS, used in the AUTOEXEC.BAT file (or as a direct command) rather than from the CONFIG.SYS file. The descriptions below are for both versions of SMARTDrive.

- You can still run the new SMARTDrive from CONFIG.SYS by using the INSTALL command in a line such as:

```
INSTALL=SMARTDRV.EXE A B 1024 /q
```

The example installs SMARTDrive for the hard disk(s), not for floppies, with 512 Kb of cache and no on-screen reminders.

To install SMARTDrive as a hard disk cache, using SMARTDRV.SYS:

1 Make sure you are using the root directory of the hard disk, and load the editor program as described earlier. Load in the CONFIG.SYS file as described.

2 Towards the end of the CONFIG.SYS file, type the line:

```
DEVICE=SMARTDRV.SYS 320 /A
```

to use the older SMARTDrive SYS file in expanded memory. Omit the /A if your computer has extended memory.

3 As before, the figure of 320 provides 320 Kb of cache. This can be increased if you have enough additional memory of either type, and a quantity of up to 2 Mb is useful.

- Some care needs to be taken with the position of the `DEVICE=RAMDRIVE.SYS` or `DEVICE=SMARTDRV.SYS` in the CONFIG.SYS file. These lines attempt to make use of memory, and unless a memory controller is already working, the commands here cannot be used. Conventional memory will be used if extended or expanded memory that has been stipulated is not present or cannot be reached for lack of a memory manager.

- For that reason, these lines that use memory management must always be placed later in the CONFIG.SYS file than the line that installs the memory manager. For example, if you have a memory manager called HIGHMEM.SYS that is installed by a line such as:

```
DEVICE=HIGHMEM.SYS
```

or:

```
DEVICE=EMM.SYS
```

then any RAMDRIVE.SYS or SMARTDRV.SYS line must be placed later in the CONFIG.SYS file.

To use SMARTDRV.EXE in the AUTOEXEC.BAT file:

1 Start an editor program and type as the filename C:\AUTOEXEC.BAT.

2 At any place in the file, preferably near the start, add the line:

```
SMARTDRV
```

3 Save the file again.

By using only the command name, you allow SMARTDrive to select the optimum operating conditions. These will depend on how much extended

RAM is present and whether or not you use Windows. The defaults are:

Available Extended RAM	SMARTDRIVE uses:	Reduced by Windows to:
1 Mb or less	All	Nil
1 to 2 Mb	1 Mb	256 Kb
2 to 4 Mb	1 Mb	512 Kb
4 to 6 Mb	2 Mb	1 Mb
More than 6 Mb	2 Mb	2 Mb

SMARTDRV.EXE options

The new SMARTDrive version contains a wider range of options than the older SMARTDRV.SYS, and it should not be used along with any other form of disk cache software.

If SMARTDRV.EXE is in a directory other than the root directory, its path must be shown. If, for example, the SMARTDRV.EXE files are in a directory called MSDOS, the command will be used in the form:

```
C:\MSDOS\SMARTDRV
```

The three main options are to show which drives will be included, the initial (main) cache size, and the Windows cache size.

- By default, SMARTDrive will cache all of your drives other than CD ROM and network. Floppy disks are cached for read-only, and hard drives are cached for both read and write.

- You can exempt floppy drives from cache use by placing a minus sign following the drive letters, so that:

```
SMARTDRV A- B-
```

will ensure that drives A and B are not cached. The hard drive C will be fully cached for both reading and writing.

The drive letter can be used alone, with the + sign or with the – sign. The drive letters are used as follows:

C	Used alone would cache this drive for reading only
C+	Would cache this drive for reading and writing
C–	Would exempt this drive from cache use

o Remember that if you omit the drive letter C completely, the C drive will be fully cached, equivalent to using **C+** in the SMARTDrive line.

The use of initial cache size and Windows cache size is unnecessary if the default values shown in the table above are satisfactory, as they usually are. Note that the values of memory shown in the table are of *available extended memory*, which is not the same as total memory or the amount of extended memory that has been added.

o For example, if you have added 1 Mb of extended memory and have used only a small amount of the 384 Kb left over from the first Mb or RAM, the default values for SMARTDrive are 1 Mb of initial cache, with Windows able to take all but 256 Kb when it needs extended memory.

The values of initial cache and the amount that is still available when Windows needs extended memory can be stipulated by you if the default values are unsatisfactory. You can, for example, use values such as:

```
SMARTDRV A- B- 1500 512
```

to specify no caching of floppy disks, an initial read/write cache of 1500 Kb for the C drive, reducing to 512 Kb when Windows needs extended memory.

o Remember that these amounts are specified in Kb (not Mb) and they must be available – if you have not enough extended memory, or have tied up extended memory in other ways such as using a RAMdisk, you cannot use such specified amounts.

If you are uncertain how much extended memory is tied up, for example by using UMB memory, it is easier and often preferable to allow the defaults to be used.

The other options are used following the slash-mark, and their defaults, where applicable, are sensible, so that you will not need to make use of the options except for special purposes.

1 /E:16 would specify that the cache moves 16 Kb at a time. The default is 8 Kb, and values used must be powers of two, such as 1, 2, 4, 8, 16, 32 etc.

2 /B:32 specifies a read-ahead buffer of 32 Kb. If a program needs to read 240 Kb from a file, SMARTDrive will read an extra 32 Kb in anticipation of the next read. The default is 16 Kb, and the number used must be a power of 2 (16, 32, 64, 128 etc.)

The other options do not concern values. They are present to enforce actions and will not necessarily be used in the SMARTDRV line of the AUTOEXEC.BAT file.

3 /C forces SMARTDrive to write all cached data to the hard disk. This option would be used in a direct command, so that if you suspected or feared that data had not been written to the disk you would type:

```
SMARTDRV /C
```

to enforce the writing of any such data.

This is seldom necessary, because writing takes place when there is no other disk activity. Use the /C option only if you are going to switch off or reboot abruptly and you are uncertain whether data has been written or not.

4 /L can be used in the SMARTDRV line of AUTOEXEC.BAT to prevent SMARTDrive from loading into UMB memory. Normally, if UMB memory is available this is where you would

want to store SMARTDrive now that the size of the program is so much greater compared with the earlier SMARTDRV.SYS.

5 /R will be used in the command SMARTDRV /R to clear the existing cache contents and restart SMARTDrive from scratch. This is not an option that you should normally need.

6 /Q can be used in the SMARTDRV line in the AUTOEXEC.BAT file to suppress the information on SMARTDrive from appearing on the screen (and slowing down the boot process).

7 /S is used while SMARTDrive is in use, in the form of the command:

```
SMARTDRV /S
```

to obtain information on the success of SMARTDrive. A typical display of the /S option is shown in Figure 5.2, showing the number of hits (when SMARTDrive has supplied data without the need to read the disk) and misses (when the disk had to be read). The status of drives is also shown.

```
Microsoft SMARTDrive Disk Cache version 4.0.091
Copyright 1991,1992 Microsoft Corp.

Room for 64 elements of 8,192 bytes each
There have been 688 cache hits
    and 450 cache misses

Cache size: 524,288 bytes
Cache size while running Windows: 524,288 bytes


            Disk Caching Status
drive    read cache    write cache    buffering
-------------------------------------------------
  C:       yes            yes            no

For help, type "Smartdrv /?".
```

Figure 5.2 The report on SMARTDrive effectiveness obtained by using SMARTDRV /S.

8 /? is used in the command:

```
SMARTDRV /?
```

to display a summary of Help on SMARTDrive and its options.

Double buffering option and disk partitions

There is another SMARTDrive option for double buffering which is of interest for older computers. To find if you need this option, make sure that you are using the directory in which SMARTDRV.EXE is located and type the command:

```
SMARTDRV                        (press Enter key)
```

This will bring up a report which, for a machine with no caching for floppy drives A and B, but with hard disk drives C and D might, for example, read:

```
                Disk Caching Status
   drive    read cache    write cache    buffering
   ------------------------------------------------
     C:        yes            yes            no
     D:        yes            yes            no
```

The 'no' answers in the *buffering* column indicate that all is well, and the BIOS chip on your computer is a modern one.

If you get 'yes' answers in the *buffering* column, alter your SMARTDRV command line in the AUTOEXEC.BAT file to read:

```
SMARTDRV (any options you need) /double_buffer
```

This will be needed only for older machines, and if you are using a 386 machine it will almost certainly not need this line. Even older 286 machines may not need it – the crucial year for the BIOS is 1987.

Another problem tied up with hardware is the use of disk partitions. Versions of MS-DOS prior to 4.0 did not provide for a hard disk of more than 32 Mb to be controlled. If your main hard disk was of more than 32 Mb, it had to be partitioned, with one portion as drive C (for example) and the other as drive D. Large hard disks might need to use three or more partitions.

- MS-DOS 5.0 can cope with any practical size of hard disk without the need for partitions, and it is often worthwhile to back up all of the hard disk and use FDISK from MS-DOS 5.0 to create a single partition on a hard disk.

- There are no problems with the use of SMARTDrive on partitioned disks when the MS-DOS FDISK utility has been used to create the partitions.

In the past, however, partitioning software has been available from other suppliers, and is often a source of conflicts. If you receive a message stating that you cannot load SMARTDrive, the problem may be due to such partitioning software.

- You can force SMARTDrive to load by specifying the /p option, but this may corrupt your hard disk if the hard disk contains more than 1024 cylinders or is not supported by the system's ROM BIOS.

- You need to make certain, if you have used partitioning software other than the FDISK utility of Microsoft, that you do not use SMARTDrive unless the hard disk corresponds to the restrictions above. Back up the disk and re-partition using FDISK if you want to make use of SMARTDrive with no restrictions.

Using RAMdisk

For many purposes, using a cache is the most efficient way of speeding up disk access for a variety of programs. If there is only a comparatively small amount of RAM (such as 320 Kb, for example, left over for loading MS-DOS into the 384 Kb of extended memory on an AT machine), the use of RAMdisk can sometimes be effective for some limited applications.

RAMdisk is RAM used as if it were a disk drive, requiring a manager to organise the signals. Time needs to be spent in copying data to the RAMdrive, but from then on it is used just like a fast disk.

- There is no automatic provision for saving the data to hard or floppy disk, however. A RAMdrive is best used for data that is copied from hard disk and does not need to be copied back.

This makes RAMdisk useful for a word-processor spelling checker, for example, copying the dictionary file to RAMdisk when the program is started and abandoning it when the program is ended (or wiping the RAMdisk clear).

○ Another example of a good use for RAMdisk is as a place for temporary files.

Many programs create temporary files as they work, and delete them afterwards. By placing such temporary files on a RAMdisk you make the programs work much faster, and the fact that the RAMdisk holds nothing after switching off the computer is no handicap. One notable exception is that some programs create no back-up files and if a fault occurs which causes a reboot the data is held only in a temporary file. WordPerfect, for example, uses this scheme which allows you to recover data after a crash. If the temporary files are deleted, so is the data.

A program which uses temporary files usually requires you to specify (in a SETUP program or in a menu) where these files are to be held, and the default is normally C:\TEMP. If you use a RAMdrive with reference letter D, you can change this temporary files line to D:\. For some programs you might need to alter a line in a batch file to:

```
SET TEMP=D:\
```

or some similar action. In general, this type of line can be placed in the AUTOEXEC.BAT file and used by many programs.

● The copying and wiping can be done by a batch file which starts the program. MS-DOS DOS-SHELL allows such preliminary and tailpiece commands to be carried out, and Windows 3.1 allows the use of object packages of commands that can work like batch files.

● Remember that RAMdisk is created by a line in the CONFIG.SYS file, which is used only as the computer boots up. You cannot cancel a

RAMdisk and regain the use of the RAM unless you edit the CONFIG.SYS file and restart the computer.

To create a RAMdisk, assuming that the C is showing:

1 Type `DIR *.SYS`. This should bring up a display of files such as in Figure 5.3. This should include RAMDRIVE.SYS. If RAMDRIVE.SYS is not present, look for it – or an equivalent such as VDISK.SYS – on your MS-DOS distribution disk. RAMDRIVE.SYS will be illustrated here.

```
Volume in drive C is IDEDISK
Volume Serial Number is 174E-A617
Directory of C:\

CONFIG.SYS          COUNTRY.SYS         DRIVER.SYS          HHSCAND.SYS
HIMEM.SYS
KEYBOARD.SYS        RAMDRIVE.SYS        SMARTDRV.SYS
        8 file(s)          76646 bytes
                        20875264 bytes free
```

Figure 5.3 A display of SYS files obtained by using `DIR *.SYS`. *Not all SYS files are essential; some of the MS-DOS set of SYS files have been deleted from this set and others have been added.*

2 Load an editor. Amstrad machines are supplied with the RPED editor, but you can use others mentioned above or the ASCII file mode of any wordprocessor. With the editor loaded, load in the document called CONFIG.SYS. This is normally found on the root directory of the hard disk.

3 This file (a typical CONFIG.SYS is shown in Figure 5.4) will contain several lines that start with the word 'DEVICE'. You need to add another by using the editor. If you are using expanded memory, place this new line near the end of the file:

```
DEVICE=RAMDRIVE.SYS 320 /A
```

If you are using extended memory on an AT machine (see later), use:

```
DEVICE=RAMDRIVE.SYS 320 /E
```

```
DEVICE=C:\MSDOS\SETVER.EXE
files=30
buffers=20
country=044,850,c:\country.sys
DEVICE=C:\MSDOS\HIMEM.SYS
INSTALL=smartdrv.exe A- B- 512 /q
SHELL=C:\MSDOS\COMMAND.COM C:\MSDOS\  /p
DOS=HIGH
stacks = 0,0
device= c:\hhscand.sys /a=280/i=3/d=1/h=4:8&:12:16/w=103/t=15
```

Figure 5.4 A reminder of a typical form of CONFIG.SYS file with DEVICE lines.

4 This will allow you to make use of 320 Kb of memory as if it were disk drive D. If you can spare more memory from expanded or extended memory, alter the figure of 320 shown above.

o If you have between 520 Kb and 1 Mb of spare extended RAM, it is usually better to use it for cache memory, as this is more efficient than RAMdisk for a large range of programs (but see later on using DOSSHELL from RAMdisk).

The CONFIG.SYS problem

The use of the cache and RAMdisk programs are set by lines in the CONFIG.SYS file, and unless you have a really large amount of RAM (and you are not using Windows) it is most unlikely that you can use both together. This makes it difficult if you want one setup for one particular program.

For example, if you want to use RAMdisk with your word processor but SMARTDrive with all of your other programs, you will need two versions of the CONFIG.SYS file, one that sets up SMARTDrive and is called CONFIG.SYS and another called CONFIG.WP which sets up RAMdrive. These files can be identical in every other respect unless you need them to be different.

The CONFIG.SYS file setting up SMARTDrive will be used normally, but to start the word processor, we need to reboot the computer with the other version. This is most easily done by using a batch file, and though it is possible to carry out the reboot automatically, this requires a little piece of program that readers are most unlikely to have, and so rebooting can be done manually (Reset button or Ctrl-Alt-Del keys).

o This has the advantage that it allows you to have second thoughts.

The CONFIG.SYS file has to be renamed as CON-FIG.OLD and the CONFIG.WP file renamed as CONFIG.SYS, before the computer is rebooted. This is done by a batch file which can be called WPPREP.BAT, containing the lines:

```
@ECHO OFF
REN C:\CONFIG.SYS C:\CONFIG.OLD
REN C:\CONFIG.WP C:\CONFIG.SYS
ECHO Now reboot and run the word processor
```

The renaming is carried out and you are reminded to run the word processor. The word processor can be run from a batch file which ends with the lines:

```
REN C:\CONFIG.SYS C:\CONFIG.WP
REN C:\CONFIG.OLD C:\CONFIG.SYS
ECHO Now reboot to restore cache program.
```

Boosting speed with MS-DOS

By far the fastest and most memory-efficient way to run programs is to run them from MS-DOS directly rather than through any form of shell, but even this action can be made faster and more efficient by the use of batch files.

o If you need to know more about batch files, take a look at the book *MS-DOS 5 File & Program Control* by Ian Sinclair, published by Sigma Press.

The batch file method of running a program is particularly useful if the program you are running is in some remote directory and needs the name of another directory for its data. For example, you might need to start the program using a command such as:

```
C:\MISCPROG\WORDS\SHRDLU \MISCDAT\WORDAT\
```

which is quite a lot to type just to start a note to the milkman. By creating a batch file called WP.BAT, which includes this line (along with any others you need) you can run the program and locate the correct data directory simply by typing WP and pressing the Enter key.

o This is not just a saving in time; it eliminates the frustration of forgetting the name of the directory or mis-spelling the command. Once the batch file is created and checked, it works unhesitatingly from then on. You can be running this program before a Windows user has found where the mouse is.

A batch file is even more useful if you need to save data to a floppy for backup after using a program, because the commands for making the backup copy can be put into the same batch file as is used to start the main program. Once again, this eliminates forgetting to back up, eliminates waste of time in typing commands, and eliminates errors due to mis-spelling once the batch file is perfected.

Running from batch files in this way provides, if used along with a disk cache, the fastest and most memory efficient way of using the computer.

o Another useful step if you have a 386 machine is to put as many of the minor memory-resident programs into the UMB region as possible. The more the main memory can be cleared, the faster most programs can run.

Using MS-DOS 5.0 macros

The use of any machine can be considerably speeded up by making use of the DOSKEY and Macro facility of MS-DOS 5.0. The sacrifice of memory that is needed for this is very small, and if your machine can make use of UMBs the programs can be run in this part of the memory, leaving the conventional memory clear.

- The DOSKEY facility becomes available when the DOSKEY utility has been run, and you would normally run this by way of a line in the AUTOEXEC.BAT file.

- The use of key macros is an interesting alternative to the use of batch files and the DOSSHELL, and can be used in conjunction with batch files to enhance their use further and to provide faster use of the machine.

Older versions of MS-DOS could make limited use of the function keys for command purposes, notably the use of F3 to repeat the most recent command, and F1 to repeat a command character by character (allowing a character to be changed).

o Version 5.0 expands this facility into a much more useful key macro system which, at its simplest, allows any command line to be recalled (not just the most recent).

The older F-key uses for F1 to F5 are still available. DOSKEY takes up only about 3 Kb of memory when installed, and is therefore not a burden on the memory.

o Even if you have no intention of using key macros, running DOSKEY allows so many useful actions that it should be used – simply to be able to recall and edit a MS-DOS command is enough justification for using DOSKEY, and you could save more time this way than by many much more elaborate methods.

Assuming that DOSKEY has been run, all commands to MS-DOS will be stored (up to a default limit of 1024 characters: more can be obtained) and can be recalled in order at any time by using the cursor up/down keys and the Page Up and Page Down keys.

o Suppose, for example that after starting the machine you used `DIR`, then `CD\MSDOS` and `DIR /W`, followed by `COPY *.SYS B:`. After using this set, the Page Down key will recall the most recent command (the COPY command) and Page Up will recall the oldest, the DIR command. The up arrow will recall an earlier command than the current one, and the down arrow key will move to a later command. Any recalled command can be run by using the Return/Enter key.

In addition to allowing old commands to be recalled in this way, DOSKEY allows for easy editing of previously-issued commands. The cursor keys can be used to move the position for editing (used alone to move by one character, with Ctrl to move by one word) or the Home and End keys can be used to move to the start or end of the line respectively. The default editing mode is overtype, meaning that a new character will replace the character under the cursor. If you want to use Insert, so that a new character will be inserted at the cursor position, press the Insert key (this will be cancelled the next time you press the Enter key). You can install DOSKEY by using:

```
DOSKEY /INSERT
```

to make insertion the default. To revert, use `DOSKEY /OVERSTRIKE`. You can use the normal delete keys on any line, and pressing Esc will delete the whole command.

The other switch options of DOSKEY are /reinstall, /bufsize, /M (or /MACROS), and /H (or /HISTORY).

1 The `/reinstall` switch will load another copy of DOSKEY into memory, allowing a new version to be used.

2 The `/bufsize` switch can be used to alter the default 1024 bytes allowed for storing DOSKEY

characters, so that `/bufsize=2048` will allocate 2048 characters for this purpose.

3 The `/dmacs` switch will display a list of all macros stored in the memory, and this can be copied to a file by using a command such as `DOSKEY /M MACFILE.DOC`, or redirected to the printer.

4 The `/H` switch similarly displays all of the stored command lines, and this also can be redirected into a file or to the printer.

The function keys F1 to F5 retain their former uses, and new uses are assigned to keys F6 to F10. These are:

F6	Put in a Ctrl-Z character
F7	Displays all stored commands
F8	Searches for a command if the first character or more has already been typed
F9	Requests a command number and displays the command
Alt-F7	Deletes all of the stored commands
Alt-F10	Deletes all stored macros

Macros

A *macro* is a file, usually held in memory, that assigns an action or set of actions to a key or key combination. In this sense, DOSSHELL uses key macros when it assigns key combinations such as Alt-A for swapping a program. The macro action of DOSKEY is invoked by using:

```
DOSKEY macroname = text
```

Each macro uses a distinctive name, and you can use single letters or longer names; the case of letters is ignored.

o Obviously, the system is most useful when one or two-letter combinations are used, since this makes for the minimum amount of typing.

Though it is possible to have macros with the same name as a DOS command (the macro will run if there is not space between the prompt and the macro name; the command will run if one or more spaces exist), this is not really advisable because of the scope that exists for confusion.

● Note that there is no provision for using the function keys for macros, because these keys are widely used by programs and they are frequently re-assigned.

● The keys which have been assigned to macro use will not retain these uses when a program is running – if you have assigned key A for providing a directory, for example, you cannot get this effect while you are running a word processor. The macro assignments will be returned into service after the program has ended and the DOS command line symbol (such as C>) re-appears.

A separate DOSKEY line is needed for each macro, so that to assign DIR to A and COPY *.* B: to B you would need to type, pressing the Enter key after each line:

```
DOSKEY A=DIR
DOSKEY B=COPY *.* B:
```

Remember that using the Alt-F10 will clear all of the macros from the memory.

o The macros are normally stored in the memory only, not on disk (unlike a batch file) and will be lost when the machine is reset or switched off, so that it can be useful to make a macros batch file (by using DOSKEY /M KEYMAC.BAT) which can be called from AUTOEXEC.BAT to re-install the macros for use on another occasion.

Such a file will consist of lines such as A=dir, and you need to use a text editor to add the DOS-KEY command at the start of each line.

The use of key macros can be easier and faster than the use of batch files for some actions, particularly when a set of actions is needed frequently. However, the key macros are stored in memory and will be deleted when the computer is switched off, unless the commands have been placed into a batch file that has then been edited as noted above. In addition, a macro cannot exceed 127 characters in length, whereas a batch file can be of any practicable length.

- To stop a macro running, Ctrl-C must be pressed as many times as there are commands in the macro.

- The use of the GOTO command in a macro is not allowed, and a macro cannot be run (though it can be created) from inside a batch file (though a batch file can be run as part of a macro command). There is nothing in a macro that corresponds to the use of ECHO OFF in the batch file.

In other ways, however, the macro language follows the methods used for batch files, though the characters that are used for some actions are different from the characters used in a batch file. All of these special macro commands start with the dollar sign and use a letter or numeral; the letter can be either upper or lower case. The full list is:

$B	Output from macro to a DOS command (like | in batch file)
$G	Redirect output, like > in a batch file
GG	Add output to end of a file, like >> in a batch file
$L	Redirect input, like < in a batch file
$T	Separator between commands in a macro (like a new line in a batch file)
$$	Dollar sign
$1 - $9	Parameters corresponding to %1 to %9 in a batch file

    $\$*$ Wildcard parameter – everything typed
                  following the macro name will be used,
                  not simply one parameter

Like batch files, macros can be typed with parameters following them, such as DX BOOK1.TXT, where DX is a macro command and the parameter is the filename BOOK.TXT.

o Any macro can be deleted by typing the line that created it without the text, so that typing DOSKEY A= will delete the macro for the letter A.

Summary of macro use

1 A macro runs much faster than a batch file, so that a macro should be used in preference to a batch file for actions such as running a program in an uncomplicated way (no elaborate setup actions), which would otherwise use short batch files.

2 Macros can be recalled only if stored in the form of a batch file.

3 Replaceable parameters and redirection can be used in macros, with a different syntax.

4 The GOTO command and the use of labels cannot be used in a macro. One macro cannot start another, though it can start a batch file.

5 Commands in a macro are displayed as they are used; there is no equivalent to @ECHO OFF.

6 The SET command can be used in a macro to create an environment variable, but a macro cannot make use of an environment variable.

Using DOSSHELL

If you need to be able to swap from one program to another, without needing to see both on screen at once, using the DOSSHELL of MS-DOS 5.0 is an excellent method. DOSSHELL is covered fully in the book quoted above, but a brief summary will be useful here for anyone who needs to know how to use DOSSHELL efficiently.

DOSSHELL is an excellent way of working with files and programs, allowing actions such as copying files to be carried out quickly and easily, with a good visual indication of what is being done.

o A special advantage that DOSSHELL has over other shell programs is that it can be used along with batch files, or can be used with its own form of batch files (the Startup command).

DOSSHELL, like other shell programs, takes up a fair amount of memory when it is working alone, but is mainly replaced when a program runs, so that its effect on the amount of memory available to the program is negligible.

In addition, DOSSHELL can carry out a lot of its file-control actions at high speed, and can be used in either text or graphics modes.

o The slowest action, as for all shell programs, is swapping programs.

Like Windows on a 286 machine, DOSSHELL allows you to switch from one program to another, with the swapped out program preserved frozen as it was when you left it. Unlike Windows, DOSSHELL makes this swap to the hard disk unless you specify otherwise.

o DOSSHELL can make its swap to RAMdrive if you specify that its TEMP file is on RAMDISK.

For example, if your AUTOEXEC.BAT file contains the line:

```
TEMP=D:\
```

and your CONFIG.SYS file has created a RAMdrive, then DOSSHELL will swap its temporary files out to RAMdrive, with a consequent saving in time, particularly in switching back.

o Using this line in AUTOEXEC.BAT will allow the RAMdrive to be used for any other programs that create temporary files, including Windows, and can therefore speed up the action of a large number of programs, not simply DOSSHELL.

Another possibility is to run DOSSHELL entirely from RAMdrive, making it very much faster in all ways, particularly in actions that involve leaving and resuming DOSSHELL.

- The speed advantage, however, is not so great as that obtained from using the RAMdisk for temporary files, though by using RAMdisk both for temporary files and for the DOSSHELL files there is a reasonable gain in speed.

- When you run DOSSHELL from a RAMdrive, you must ensure that all of the files named DOS-SHELL, along with the DOSSWAP.EXE file, are transferred.

This is best done by using lines in the AUTOEXEC.BAT file:

```
COPY C:\MSDOS\DOSSHELL.* D:\
COPY C:\MSDOS\DOSSWAP.EXE D:\
D:\DOSSHELL
```

These lines copy the files and then start DOS-SHELL from the RAMdrive (D in this example).

One point to watch is that you sometimes want to customise DOSSHELL to your own requirements. If DOSSHELL is always run from the RAMdrive, these alterations will only ever be temporary, and DOS-SHELL will always start in the mode that it used when the files were last used from the hard disk.

A way out of this is to run DOSSHELL from a batch file whose last line is:

```
COPY D:\DOSSHELL.INI C:\MSDOS
```

so that the DOSSHELL.INI file which keeps track of changes, is always saved back to the hard disk.

On the other hand, you might prefer to keep an unchanging version on the hard disk, allowing you to make temporary changes only in the running version. This avoids the need to have to change back to your preferred setup each time you start DOSSHELL.

The gains that can be derived from using RAMdrive for temporary files and/or running DOS-SHELL from RAMdrive do not apply when a new program is started up, because each new program will have to be read from the hard disk. In addition, there is a limit to how much can be kept in RAMdrive, and using RAMdrive for temporary files carries the risk that you might run out of space for these files.

- When this happens, DOSSHELL will not allow you to swap out of a program and you will have to close the program down in order to run another one.

- DOSSHELL will also benefit from the use of a large cache. This solution is not quite so fast as the use of RAMdrive, using a cache which permits caching of written data will allow temporary files to be written and read faster than if the hard disk alone were being used.

Speed and GUI use

GUI is the buzzword for *Graphical User Interface*, meaning a display of windows where icons are selected by a mouse. The established GUI for the PC is Windows, and at the time of writing version 3.1 was available with distinct advantages in speed and facilities as compared to version 3.0.

All GUI programs form another layer of program between the user and MS-DOS. The benefits in terms of juggling with several programs and using similar (often clumsy) mouse actions for all, have to be balanced against slower running (sometimes exasperatingly slow) and the need for large memory resources.

o One commentator has said (jokingly of course) that Windows always needs 2 Mb more than you ever have.

You should not be carried away by advertising and bandwagon effects. If you spend most of the day with the MS-DOS version of WordPerfect in use, for example, adding Windows does absolutely nothing for you unless you really want to buy the WordPerfect for Windows version.

- Contrary to what advertisers preach, software does not really go out of date. All that can happen is that you may feel that a new version offers advantages that are not available on your version.

- Programs like word processors, spreadsheets and databases have been around for a long time, and really innovative additions are now rare. The spectacular displays of the Windows versions may not appeal to you, and many users feel that they are a distraction.

- In addition, for anyone who knows the keyboard layout, using keys for control of such programs is much faster than working with a mouse. A mouse is virtually an essential for graphics programs such as Paint and CAD programs, extremely useful for DOSSHELL, but much less useful for text-based programs.

For anyone wanting to maintain high speed and efficient use of memory, but with the use of the mouse for selecting programs and file actions, it would be very hard to beat the DOSSHELL of MS-DOS 5.0. DOSSHELL even allows you to switch from one program to another without shutting down programs.

Other Windows assistants

If you are content to run Windows in its standard mode (either on a 286 machine or on a 386 machine which has 2 Mb or less), it will run faster.

All you lose is the ability to keep more than one program running (as distinct from suspended) at a time, and the ability to use non-Windows programs in separate windows on 386 machines.

- o Users of 286 machines cannot run non-Windows programs in separate windows in any case.

Windows requires so much memory that it rules out useful ways of speeding up its actions, such as placing temporary files on RAMdrive. By far the best advice for fast use of Windows is to extend the memory to as much as the machine will bear.

- Using 8 Mb of extended memory, for example, on a fast 386 machine can make Windows decidedly more pleasant to work with, but you should remember that almost any scheme would work well with so much memory. You could, for example, create a large RAMdrive and load in DOSSHELL with all your program files into it.

- Using SMARTDrive for a 1 Mb cache will significantly improve the performance of any recent version of Windows. This does not take 1 Mb away from Windows because SMARTDrive will co-operate with Windows in the use of memory.

In general, using Windows 3.1 with adequate memory and a SMARTDrive cache in use will allow it to run faster on program swapping than DOS-SHELL run from the hard disk.

- One of the most serious bottlenecks for Windows is the graphics screen of the PC. Some graphics cards (such as the ATI 8514 ULTRA) claim to run considerably faster than a conventional VGA card and hence speed up the use of Windows considerably.

- Using a monochrome display is one simple way of speeding up graphics displays, since so much less information needs to be handled. There is also a bonus of better resolution unless the colour monitor you were using was a very costly type (£750 or more).

- Do not run Windows using a Super VGA (SVGA) type of display. The appearance may be beautiful, but SVGA is slower than VGA because so many more items have to be manipulated each time a screen view is changed.

- There is a piece of software, More Windows, from Ctrl Alt Deli, that not only provides more of Windows on screen, using a SVGA type of driver, it also speeds up displays by adding a cache for video displays. This is one of the few instances of having your cake and eating it.

In addition to having as much memory as you can install and the installation of SMARTDrive, there are a lot of minor ways in which your use of Windows can be accelerated. These are:

1 Ensuring that memory is not overloaded with unnecessary resident programs.

2 Ensuring that the hard disk is cleared of unnecessary files.

3 Ensuring that the hard disk is kept in a compressed state.

4 Ensuring that Windows swap files are used efficiently.

The first, second and fourth of these points will be dealt with here and the third will be noted in Chapter 6.

Making deletions

You ought to delete from your hard disk:

1 Any Windows files that were installed automatically by the Windows Setup program but which are not needed either now or in the future: the games programs are the usual target in this respect.

2 Any other program files, text files, or utilities that you no longer need or use.

3 Any temporary files that are left on your hard disk when your computer fails unexpectedly. This includes the Windows application swap files (see later for explanation).

o In particular, you should delete any files you find in your TEMP directory after ending a Windows session. This is the directory that all programs use to store temporary files, and there should never be any files remaining after programs have ended. Never delete files in the TEMP directory when programs are still running (or suspended).

Any files that start with the characters ~WOA are temporary application swap files created when Windows runs in standard mode. These are usually deleted automatically but might remain on the hard disk if Windows has stopped running unexpectedly. They can safely be deleted if Windows is not running.

The file WIN386.SWP is a temporary Windows swap file which is created in 386 enhanced mode (if no permanent file exists – see later), and should be deleted on exit from Windows. It can be deleted if Windows is not running.

o Do *not* delete files named 386SPART.PAR or SPART.PAR. These are permanent swap files – see later.

You can also free up disk space by deleting one or more of the following list of Windows facilities. You need to decide for yourself which are unnecessary to your uses of Windows – for many users the wallpaper files come into this category.

1 Files with the .BMP filename extension are used for desktop wallpaper and contribute nothing useful to Windows, though some of them take a considerable amount of space.

2 SOL.EXE, SOL.HLP, WINMINE.EXE, WIN-MINE.HLP, WINMINE.EXE, WINMINE.HLP are games files and could have been rejected on Setup.

3 You might also find that you do not need some Windows accessories such as the files that start with the letters shown below:

PBRUSH	The Paintbrush accessory
WRITE	The Write word processor
CALENDAR	The Calendar accessory
CALC	The pop-up calculator
CARDFILE	The Cardfile database
TERMINAL	The data terminal accessory
RECORDER	The macro recorder accessory
CLOCK.EXE	The clock accessory

In all the list above, there may be several files with the same main name but with different extensions such as EXE, HLP and so on. If you want to delete an accessory, delete all the files with the same main name.

4 EMM386.EXE: the expanded-memory emulator should be deleted only if you are not likely ever to need expanded memory or UMB use. Delete this only if you are quite desperately short of disk space.

After deleting files

After you have deleted files you do not need, you should leave Windows and run the CHKDSK utility to clean up lost clusters of data that are taking up space on the hard disk.

o Information can become lost when a program stops running unexpectedly, leaving fragments of files on the hard disk without having saved them or deleted them.

After a long period of use these fragments will take up an appreciable amount of disk space. Using CHKDSK /F finds and fixes any lost clusters. If these are likely to be of text (abandoned when a word processor failed), CHKDSK can convert them to usable text files that you can examine, add to other files or delete as required. Program file fragments can never be used in this way.

o You *must* ensure that Windows is not running when you use CHKDSK /F, and obviously you must never run CHKDSK /F from Windows. This would result in CHKDSK mopping up your Windows swapped data files. You should, in fact, clear the memory of all shell programs (other than COMMAND.COM), and including DOS-SHELL.

You should always run CHKDSK /F:

1 Before using any hard disk compressing utility.

2 If any program stops running unexpectedly.

Windows swap files

When you switch from one Windows program to another, Windows makes use of a *swap file* to hold the program which is suspended, and in the course of a Windows session several files may be held in this way. Windows uses two types of swap files, depending on whether you are using 386 enhanced mode (possible only if you are using a 386 machine with 2 Mb or more), or standard mode (used on 286 machines and on 386 machines with less than 2 Mb of RAM).

In standard mode, Windows creates a temporary swap file each time you start a non-Windows program and switch away from it. This file is called an *application swap file* and it moves some or all of the program from the memory into a swap file on the hard disk, releasing memory for the program you want to switch to. When you stop using a program, Windows will delete any swap files it created for that program.

- Programs that are designed to be run under Windows are swapped to extended memory rather than to hard disk, provided that there is extended memory available.

- This system of using application swap files for specific programs is not used when Windows is running in 386 enhanced mode.

The number of application swap files Windows can create is decided by the amount of free disk space; the files are hidden files with names that start with the characters ~WOA. If you use DOS-SHELL with the Show Hidden/System Files option selected, you can see such files if they still exist.

Windows puts these files in the directory specified by the swap-disk setting in the SYSTEM.INI file.

- If there is no swap-disk setting line, Windows will place the files in the directory specified by the TEMP environment variable in your AUTOEXEC.BAT file. For example, if you have used:

```
TEMP=C:\WINDOWS\TEMP
```

the swap files will be placed in this directory.

- If there is no TEMP line in the AUTOEXEC.BAT file, Windows places swap files in the root directory of the first hard disk drive. The location that Windows uses to store these application swap files will determine how long it takes to switch to and from non-Windows programs.

- Note that this does *not* affect the timing for switching to and from programs that are designed to run entirely under Windows, such as EXCEL, WordPerfect for Windows, COREL DRAW, PageMaker and so on.

It is a considerable temptation to try to speed up swap files by using RAMdisk. This is not as useful as it seems because the RAMdisk makes use of memory that otherwise would be better used by Windows.

○ Use RAMdisk only if you have a very large amount of memory to spare – this is unusual.

The best other option for the swap-disk setting is the fastest disk you have, which for most users is simply the C: drive. This makes it unnecessary to do anything, since it is the default.

Enhanced mode swap files

When Windows can run in 386 enhanced mode, it also makes use of swap files, but in a different way. The files are still hidden files on the hard disk, and the amount of space on the hard disk determines how many files you can juggle at one time. The Setup program will set up a permanent swap file if it can, and if no permanent swap file is set up Windows will create a temporary swap file whenever it is started in 386 enhanced mode.

○ A permanent swap file is faster because it does not need to be created each time Windows is started up.

A permanent Windows swap file consists in fact of two files called SPART.PAR and 386SPART.PAR. SPART.PAR is a read-only file and is located in the WINDOWS directory. 386SPART.PAR is a hidden file and is located in the root directory of (usually) the hard drive. Neither of these files must *ever* be deleted, moved or renamed.

You would normally not need to make any changes in these permanent swap files for a 386 machine, except possible to create a larger swap file if you were using large programs. This can be done from within Windows by using the Control Panel, selecting the 386 Enhanced icon.

o The menu to select is Change in Virtual Memory, which allows you to specify drive, type and size (in Kb).

6 More Hardware

Using the hard disk

The hard disk can be used as an extension of memory, and many programs do this automatically. WordPerfect and WordStar, for example, work with some of a document held in the memory and the rest on the disk (using swap files). This allows these word processors to work with documents of almost any size, practically up to half of the capacity of the disk.

- Use of a disk in this way is often described as *virtual memory*, and the 80386/80486 type of chips are organised so as to allow the use of huge amounts of virtual memory, up to 4 Gb (1 Gb=1024 Mb).

- The important point here is that the 80386 or 80486 chip itself can make use of virtual memory, swapping bytes between disk and memory, irrespective of the software being run.

All of this, however, depends on a suitable operating system being in use. MS-DOS still has to be compatible with the 8088 and 8086 type of chips, in which virtual memory was not implemented, so that virtual memory cannot be used when MS-DOS controls the 80386 or 80486 chip.

o It is certain that the later operating system called NT, designed for the 80386 and later chips, will allow the full capabilities of these chips to be used while still being capable of running familiar DOS programs.

At present, however, virtual memory of this type is implemented by software, a much slower operation than the use of address numbers to locate bytes on the disk.

Hard disk storage

Switching data between the hard disk and the memory is not a fast action, and it is slowed down considerably if the disk storage is not efficient. When a hard disk is being used in this way, a lot of files are being saved and later deleted.

- Each time a file is deleted, the space on the disk that it used becomes available for other files to be saved, but these files are not likely to be of the same size as the deleted file.

- The result is that some of the space is used, and some is not. The space that is not used can be locked out of use for a considerable time until files around it are deleted.

- A smaller file will fit into a large space, but when you save a larger file, part of the file goes into the vacant space and part goes wherever else is available. You can even get a file split up into many parts with pieces fitting into a set of spaces that were liberated by small deleted files.

- Invariably, some space becomes impossible to use because its size is smaller than the minimum space that the computer looks for when it tries to save a file on the disk.

After some time, your hard disk gives a passable imitation of a piece of Emmenthal cheese, thoroughly riddled with gaps. In addition, some files may be split into many pieces. The effect is to make disk saving and loading very much slower than it could be if each file followed each other file in a smooth sequence, and with all the bytes of one file placed in sequence on the disk. This is the way that files will be stored when they are first saved on a new disk.

A disk compressor is a program which does just this re-organisation, shuffling the files about so as to pack the disk more efficiently. If this is done correctly the result is a hard disk which performs faster and more efficiently. If things go wrong, the result is a totally scrambled disk.

○ One of the things that can go wrong is a power failure when you are in the middle of it all, another is embarking on this sort of action when you have insufficient time and have to switch off half-way.

You can also get into trouble if the disk contains any damaged files when you start the process. As usual, the experienced and knowledgeable user gets the best of it.

● MS-DOS 5.0 does not contain a disk compressor utility, a puzzling omission. DR-DOS 6.0 contains the DISKOPT utility, and there is an excellent COMPRESS utility in the PC-Tools set.

● Some caution is needed, though, because a hard disk is a precious commodity due to the value of the files that it holds.

● This means that you have to use any hard-disk utility with caution. Used correctly, you could considerably improve the running of your hard disk. Used incorrectly, you could possibly lose the use of the hard disk, and have to start all over again with it.

Analysing hard disk use

After a period of intensive use, as has been described here, the hard disk contains a lot of fragmented files and a lot of unused and unusable space.

● A hard disk, by its nature, suffers from this problem much more than a floppy, because so many files are likely to be stored, erased and altered on a hard disk.

● In addition, one important reason for using a hard disk is speed of access to files. A disk that contains heavily-fragmented files will work considerably slower than one which is well-organised.

All Toolbox programs, such as PC-Tools, provide routines for checking the health of your disk, allowing you to determine when the time has come to compress the disk. In addition, a check can show if there are any bad sectors on the disk, indicating damage that might indicate possible problems on the way. All such programs will also take particular care of the hidden files, IO.SYS and MSDOS.SYS (or their equivalents) which must usually be stored at specific parts of a disk.

o Never be tempted to move these files to other directories – they must stay where they were placed when the disk was formatted. MS-DOS 5.0 is more forgiving about the placing of these files than older DOS versions but you should be careful about them nevertheless. It is better not to make use of any software option that allows these files to be visible in a DIR listing.

Figure 6.1 shows a display, with the results of some recent deletions obvious, and a few sectors scattered.

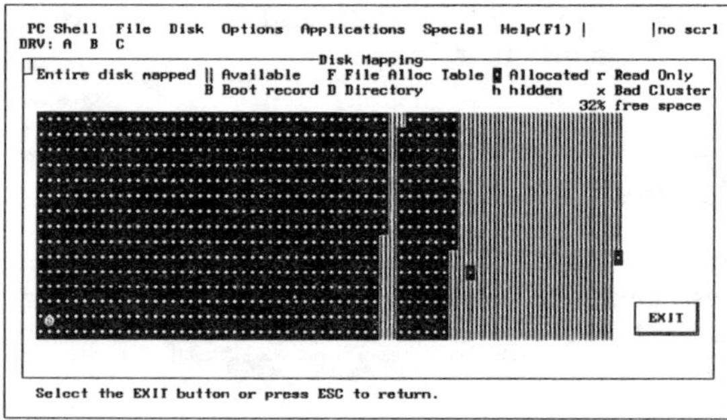

Figure 6.1   A display from PC-Tools showing disk fragmentation.

This shows the disk use, not how much fragmentation exists in individual files.

File fragmentation is reported when the Compress option of PC-Tools is used, and there is provision for looking at the fragmentation report only, without compressing the disk.

- This is important, because the compression of a hard disk can take several hours for a large-capacity disk on a slow computer and it may not be convenient to carry out at the time when you are examining for fragmentation.

- In addition, disk compression must never be carried out unless you have adequate backups, of all files. This does not infer that compression programs are inherently unsafe, only that they might be interrupted by a power cut, which would leave the contents of the hard disk fairly thoroughly scrambled.

- *Never* run any kind of disk compression programs from within Windows, DOSSHELL or any other shell type of program. End your use of such programs before starting disk compression activities.

Before compressing a disk, it is always wise to run the CHKDSK utility in the form:

```
CHKDSK /F
```

to gather up and eliminate any file fragments that might otherwise clutter up the disk. This point was also noted in Chapter 5.

- Remember that CHKDSK /F also must never be run from within any shell program, such as Windows, DOSSHELL or DESQview. Run CHKDSK from MS-DOS when all shell programs have been ended (not just suspended).

- It is safer to keep a floppy with a very simple CONFIG.SYS and AUTOEXEC.BAT, which will not load any memory-resident programs other than KEYB or (if needed) MOUSE. Use this floppy to reboot from before running CHKDSK /F.

Selecting disk compression with PC-Tools (or using their Compress utility from DOS) produces the display as indicated in Figure 6.2, with actions on the F4 - F8 keys.

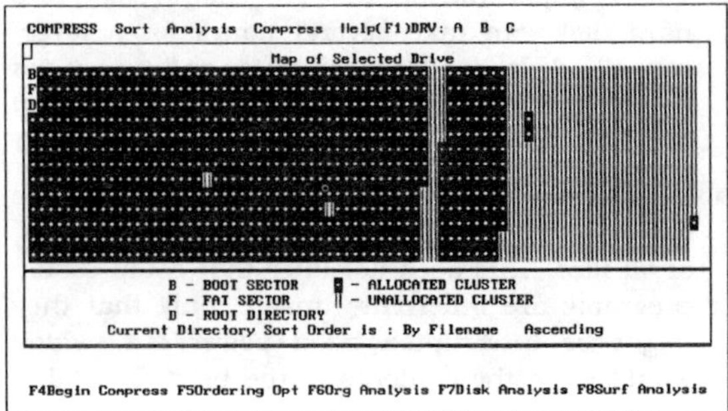

Figure 6.2 The disk compression display.

1 Press or select F7 (or select Analysis from the top line, then Disk Analysis) for a preliminary analysis. You will be asked to specify a sorting order for directories – the default is by name and ascending. This action takes time, and results in a display such as that of Figure 6.3.

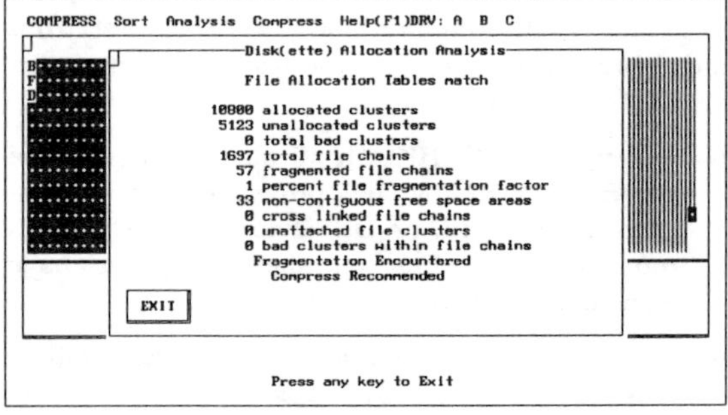

Figure 6.3 The display after analysis, recommending compression.

2 The report will note the extent of fragmentation and recommend compression if it is needed.

3 Another option, File Analysis, is obtained by selecting Analysis from the top-line menu (there is no F-key option). The results are as shown in Figure 6.4, using one screen for each directory. The percentage of fragmentation indicates the need for compression.

```
COMPRESS  Sort  Analysis  Compress  Help(F1)DRV: A  B  C
                       ─File Allocation Analysis─
Path=C:\PCTOOLS
Name          Clusters Areas   Pct   Name          Clusters Areas   Pct
.        <DIR>    2    2    50%   PCB2.EXE          6    1    0%
..       <DIR>                    PCB3.EXE         15    1    0%
PCSHELL.EXE      54    8    94%   PCB4.EXE          7    1    0%
PCSHELL.OVL     112    9    93%   PCB5.EXE         12    1    0%
FORMAT.BAT        1    1     0%   PCB6.COM          4    1    0%
PCRUN.COM         2    1     0%   PCBDIR.COM        6    1    0%
PCSETUP.EXE      34    1     0%   README.TXT        7    1    0%
PCSETUP.CFG       1    1     0%   PCSHELL.HLP      21    1    0%
PCFORMAT.COM      9    1     0%   PC-CACHE.COM     14    1    0%
MI.COM            3    1     0%   PC-CACHE.SYS      1    1    0%
PCBACKUP.EXE     47    1     0%   MIRROR.COM        8    1    0%
PCBACKUP.HLP     15    1     0%   REBUILD.COM       9    1    0%
PCB1.EXE          6    1     0%   KILL.EXE          1    1    0%

  PREV DIR      NEXT DIR      FIRST DIR      LAST DIR      EXIT

        Press Esc key or F3 key to terminate File Analysis
```

Figure 6.4 The file analysis display, showing the extent of fragmentation of files.

4 The third analysis option is Surface Analysis, which produces a report such as that of Figure 6.5 (shown part-way through). This checks all of the disk clusters, looking for clusters that are marginally effective or bad. A report can be delivered optionally to the printer or to a disk file.

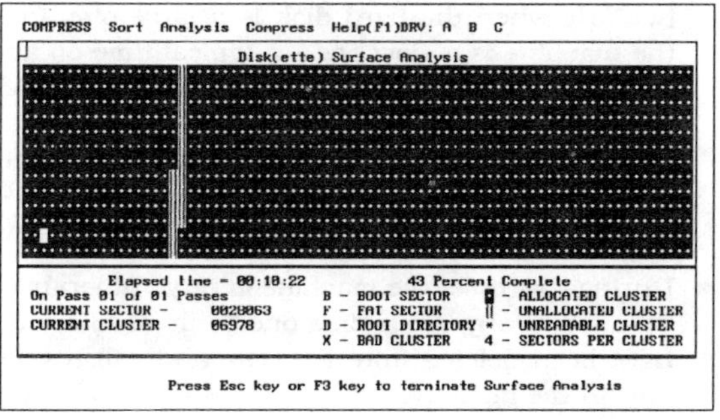

Figure 6.5 Surface analysis of a hard disk, illustrated partly completed.

- Surface analysis takes a *considerable* time, almost as long as a full compression of the disk.

- One useful feature is that a cluster which is found to be bad will have its data shifted (if in use) before being marked as bad.

- The screen display has to be changed several times to accommodate the number of clusters in a hard disk.

Compressing the disk

It can be useful to compress the hard disk at intervals – some users do so each week, but monthly is a better interval for a machine that is used at a reasonable level. An analysis will indicate when compression is needed.

- It is important to be clear about what compression involves. Files have to be read from the disk into the remaining memory of the computer, and then deleted from the disk so that other files can be put into their place.

- This starts at the files at the beginning of the disk tracks and shuffles the files around until there is a minimum of lost space and no fragmented files.

- All of this can take a considerable time, particularly when the hard disk is a large one and the machine is a slow one – a typical time on an XT machine with a slow 32 Mb disk would be of the order of an hour. A fast AT machine with a comparatively small hard disk of 20 Mb might complete the task in under ten minutes, by contrast.

- During this time, the machine is very vulnerable, because at any given time one or more files will have been deleted from the disk and will reside only in the memory.

- In addition, the correct position of the files on the disk is also held in the memory, so that if anything should happen, the chances of recovering the data would be fairly slim.

- The most likely upset is a power cut (ever seen a petition in favour of building a new power station?), but there are always people around who will switch off a machine that doesn't seem to be doing much.

To use the COMPRESS option of PC-Tools:

1 Select the hard disk drive.

2 Select Applications and then Compress Disk.

3 From the menu on the top line, select Compress.

4 The Compress menu appears. You are warned not to use memory-resident programs other than PC-Tools.

5 Directories are sorted prior to compressing. During compression, the screen shows the files that are being moved.

6 You can stop the action at any stage by pressing the Esc key.

- It is useful to be able to stop compression, since this allows the work to be done in stages.

- Compression of a disk that is already reasonably well-organised is very much faster than for a completely fragmented disk.

There are several other precautions that must be taken and notes to remember after compressing a disk.

1 You must *always* reboot the machine, either by Ctrl-Alt-Del or by switching off and then on again.

2 You will have lost any trace of deleted files, so that no form of file recovery can possibly work after compression.

3 There may still be some gaps in the disk, caused because of files with hidden or system attributes which have not been moved.

o Most disk-compression utilities will try to place essential DOS files on the lowest numbered sectors of the disk for fastest access. You must never try to relocate these files (such as IO.SYS and MSDOS.SYS).

Disk-file compressors

A form of software that is becoming more popular is the disk-file compressor. This does not alter the way that the disk is organised, but uses software to reduce the size of each file before it is stored on the disk, making use of the familiar methods that have been used for some time in archiving programs. The number of files that can be stored in a given space can usually be (at least) doubled in this way. Files are expanded to normal size when they are being retrieved from the disk.

o The downside is that the coding of files for storage and the decoding for their use takes time and will increase the overall time needed for disk operations. There is a small compensation in saving time by having smaller files to load and store, but overall there is a speed penalty.

Two of the best known of these programs are Stacker, which is recognised by Microsoft in its Windows documentation, and SuperStor, a reduced version of which is incorporated into the DR-DOS 6.0 package.

Both of these packages allow you to split a hard drive into two (or more) partitions, so that you can reserve one partition for compressed files and the other for uncompressed files. These partitions will use separate drive letters such as, for example, C: (compressed) and D: (uncompressed).

● The CONFIG.SYS file must never be compressed, because it has to be read before any other software is installed. All file-compressor programs allow for CONFIG.SYS to be left uncompressed.

● If you use a swap file with Windows (see Chapter 5), you must set up the swap file on the uncompressed drive, never on the compressed drive, and ensure that the size of this partition is large enough.

When setting up Stacker or SuperStor you should specify at least one megabyte of uncompressed disk space for storing system files, but this is not enough if you are using Windows swap files.

- The recommendation is to use uncompressed disk space equal to at least twice the amount of system memory. For example, if your system has 3 Mb of memory, you should leave at least 6 Mb of uncompressed disk space.

- You need not use SMARTDrive to cache the compressed drive, only the uncompressed drive. The SMARTDRV.EXE line of CONFIG.SYS can specify which drives to cache if you are using the version of SMARTDrive that comes with Windows 3.1 (see Chapter 5).

For example, if drive C is compressed and D is uncompressed, the CONFIG.SYS line:

```
DEVICE=\WINDOWS\SMARTDRV.EXE C- D+
```

will ensure that SMARTDrive works only on the D: drive and will cache both read and write actions. Older versions of SMARTDrive do not permit the use of the C- D+ options, and by default SMARTDrive would cache all hard disk drive letters.

Using video memory

Video boards, particularly the VGA type, make use of memory, and some of this memory can be used if not required. The boards allocate some memory for text and further memory for graphics, and it is the allocation for graphics that can be used if graphics are not required.

- This rules out taking video memory if you are running any form of graphics shell, such as Windows. Even a word processor such as WordPerfect will need to make use of graphics if you use the page preview feature (as you normally would).

- Using video memory is most useful for large text-based programs such as dBASE 4, provided that no graphs need to be drawn. Many other programs such as accounts programs, time organisers, editors, communications, estimating systems, label printers, payroll packages, electronics programs, genealogy, retail software, etc. also can run with no need for graphics.

For a VGA video board, as much as 96 Kb extra RAM can be made available, and by using a suitable memory manager this amount of memory can be added to conventional memory, allowing you a conventional RAM space of 736 Kb.

o Video RAM is not available from CGA or Hercules mono graphics boards. A few utilities exist that allow you to make use of the video RAM, which is unused when a VGA card is used with a mono monitor.

Neither MS-DOS nor DR-DOS make provision for using memory in the video board, but Quarterdeck, always the leaders in memory usage, can provide the programs called VIDRAM as part of their QRAM (for 286) or QEMM (for 386) collections. VIDRAM can be used on PC/XT machines (8088 or 8086 chip) also.

To use VIDRAM, the program should be placed in the root directory of the hard drive, and a line added into the AUTOEXEC.BAT file:

```
VIDRAM ON
```

which will activate VIDRAM when the machine is booted.

o Remember that this option is suitable only if you seldom run graphics programs.

You can switch the use of video memory off by using:

```
VIDRAM OFF
```

when you need to make use of a graphics program, but this command should be issued from MS-DOS directly, not from any shell program.

The other way of using VIDRAM is to run all your non-graphics programs from their own batch files, using VIDRAM ON at the start of the file (ahead of the name of the program) and VIDRAM OFF at the end of the file (following the program name).

o This allows video memory to be used only for those programs that will not make any access to graphics. You could reverse this system and use VIDRAM ON in the AUTOEXEC.BAT file, with VIDRAM OFF at the start of each graphics programs and VIDRAM ON at the end.

Faster booting

There are improvements in speed and other facilities that are available only by your choice of hardware and not from any software add-ons. It may be that your present computer permits such actions and you have not made use of them, or that nothing of the sort is available, in which case you know what to look for in your next machine.

- If your machine uses a Turbo switch, ensure that this is always set to the faster speed. The switch was originally incorporated in case some programs could not run at the higher speed, but nowadays it is most unlikely that you would be using such programs. A lot of machines provide for the Turbo switch to be disregarded and the machine permanently set to the higher speed.

- Many machines now on offer at low prices incorporate the facilities mentioned here, so that it is likely that many readers of this book will be able to improve speed and memory use by taking advantage of what is available.

- Some chipsets can boot very much faster than others, and in this respect, the Headland set with the Quantel BIOS is noticeably faster than most others.

All of the actions described below are available, if implemented, from the CMOS SETUP of an AT machine. There are various methods of reaching this CMOS SETUP menu, such as pressing the Del key while the machine is on its self-test, or booting the machine with the keyboard lock on. The manual (or leaflet) that comes with the computer should state how the CMOS SETUP is reached if neither of these actions works. You may have to press another key, such as the F2 key, to get to CMOS SETUP after interrupting the boot process.

o The facilities that are on offer vary greatly from one type of chipset to another, so that the examples, from a MicroSurgeons Swift 386 with Chips & Technologies SCAT-SX chipset, should be taken as general advice only.

The usual options allow for Standard CMOS setup, Advanced CMOS setup and Advanced Chipset setup. Of these, the standard CMOS setup deals with date and time, disk and keyboard, and is not involved in the actions described here. It is the Advanced CMOS and Chipset options that are of interest.

The set of options offered is typically:

```
Typematic rate programming
Typematic rate delay
Typematic rate chars/sec
Above 1 Mb memory test
Memory test tick sound
Memory parity error check
Hit DEL message display
Hard disk type 47 RAM area
Wait for F1 if any error
System boot-up Num Lock
Numeric processor test
Floppy drive seek at boot
System boot-up sequence
System boot-up CPU speed
Turbo switch function
Password checking option
Video ROM shadow C000, 32K
Adaptor ROM shadow C800,32K
Adaptor ROM shadow D000,32K
Adaptor ROM shadow D800,32K
Adaptor ROM shadow E000,32K
Adaptor ROM shadow E800,32K
System ROM shadow F000,64K
```

o Most of these options are labelled as Enable or Disable, and the change is made by pressing the Page Up or Page Down keys.

Disabling the *memory test* above 1 Mb will save a considerable amount of time on a machine with several megabytes of extended memory. The memory test really need not be run each time the computer is booted (have you ever seen it fail?), and is best reserved for any time when you have doubts about some recently-installed memory.

Similarly, disabling the *memory parity check* also saves time. On some machines, the parity bit is implemented by a separate set of memory chips and if these are not present the test must certainly not be used. As before, the parity check is really superfluous on a modern machine except where memory has just been added and might be doubtful.

The *numeric processor test* is not needed if no numeric processor has been installed (see later), and omitting this test will save some time even if the co-processor is in place – like memory, it need be tested only when it is first installed.

Disabling the *floppy drive seek at boot time* takes a few seconds off the boot-up time, because the system can then boot straight from the hard disk.

o On some machines, using this option makes it impossible to boot from a floppy, and the option must be reset before a floppy can be used for booting.

On the C&T set, using this option will still allow you to boot from a floppy if the hard disk fails. In conjunction with this option, using a *system boot-up sequence* of `C:,A:` ensures that the hard drive (or any other drive you nominate) will be tried first to boot the machine. The default is `A:,C;,` and `C:,A;` is the other option. Only the drive letters shown in the Simple Setup page will appear in this option.

The *Turbo switch function* should be disabled if you also set the *System boot-up speed* as high; this avoids wasting time because the Turbo switch has been inadvertently pushed.

o Avoid all *password protection* systems unless you feel that they are essential.

If you forget a password you can find yourself locked out of using the machine, and it is by no means easy to get out of it (by disconnecting the CMOS battery momentarily, then rebooting and selecting BIOS defaults for the CMOS memory). The need to type a password increases the time needed to boot the computer, particularly if your spelling is poor.

The *ROM shadow* options should be used where applicable if your machine has enough memory to allow this to be done. On a machine with only 1 Mb there are better uses for the 384 Kb of extended RAM which would be used in this way, but using 64 Kb of this RAM as a shadow for System ROM will significantly speed up the machine.

o This is because the ROM memory is slow acting, and by copying the ROM contents to RAM and using fast-acting RAM in place of ROM, the processor can execute its actions much faster.

Use the *Adaptor ROM shadow* options only if you know what addresses are used for adaptor ROMs, and have enough memory to spare for this type of use. You can use the reports of memory analysers to find these addresses.

o Remember that if you make use of this action on a machine with only 386 Kb or extended RAM it will be impossible to use EMM386.EXE and to gain access to upper memory blocks.

The Advanced Chipset features are less likely to be useful, but they should be checked. A typical set is:

>   Low CPU clock speed
>   BUS clock select
>   Additional RAM wait state
>   CAS extended wait state
>   Extended memory boundary
>   Global EMS memory
>   EMS I/O port access
>   EMS Page Registers

There will be a gain in speed if the *Additional RAM wait state* and *CAS extended wait state* options are selected as 'disabled'.

- Where a chipset offers options on the use of extended and expanded memory, it is usually better to disable these options, because they are likely to conflict with your use of software memory controllers, sometimes in a very puzzling way.

- Many programs assume that your machine is a perfectly standard IBM clone, and the use of some advanced chipset options can cause conflicts.

Speeding CAD and spreadsheets

The Intel chipset, whether it is based on the old 8088, the superior 8086, or any of the later advanced chips such as 80286, 80386 or 80486, allows for the use of co-processors, chips which can take over the running of the computer from the main microprocessor. The only chip that is found to any extent as a co-processor, however, is the maths co-processor, such as the 8087, 80287 or 80387.

The 8087 was originally an expensive chip, costing in the region of £100, whose specialised action is floating-point mathematical actions for the 8088 or 8086 chips.

- The normal microprocessor is capable of very limited arithmetical actions using integer numbers: that is, numbers which contain no fractions and have a limited range of value.

- Numbers which contain fractions or are outside the range of the integers that the 8088, 8086 or later 80286 and 80386 can use have to be dealt with by the use of software.

The use of software introduces two penalties. One is that the speed with which these floating-point numbers can be manipulated is much lower than for integers, because each action carried out with these floating-point numbers (so called to distinguish them from fractions in which the decimal point is always at a fixed position) requires a large number of software program steps to carry out.

o During the time that each arithmetic action with a floating-point number is being executed, the main microprocessor is tied up, slowing down the overall action of the computer.

The other problem is that the storage of a floating-point number in binary code form is almost always approximate, so that the results of arithmetic using floating-point numbers will be incorrect unless the results are rounded up or down – and rounding requires some rather clever (and slow-acting) software instructions.

o A common test is an action such as 9/11 + 2/11, which will with some software not result in 1.00 but in 0.9999999999. This is a problem of binary code rather than of the microprocessor, but it adds to the amount of software that has to be executed in order to deal with floating-point arithmetic.

The 8087 is a chip which deals with floating-point actions using a combination of hardware and built-in software routines.

o The important point, however, is that it can work in parallel alongside the main processor, interrupting the main processor only when it needs to be fed with data or needs to pass results back into the main system.

The use of the 8087 on the XT type of machine will therefore speed up working with floating-point numbers by an amazingly large factor. This is particularly true of the XT type of machine with an 8088 chip running at a low clock speed of around 4 MHz. Later 8088 clones have used faster speeds, and most of the 8086 machines use a clock speed of 8 MHz. The use of the 8087 is not quite such a marked advantage for the 8086 machines, but it still offers a very considerable improvement in speeds on these machines.

The speed improvement, however, depends on the type of software that is being used.

- Programs such as word processors make no use of floating-point arithmetic, so that the fitting of the 8087 to your XT machine will have no noticeable effect if you use the machine exclusively for word processing.

- If, however, you use large spreadsheets such as Lotus 1-2-3, then the effect of the added 8087 is very dramatic, obviating the annoying delays that can occur even with relatively small worksheets when every cell of the spreadsheet has to be recalculated following an entry.

- The same advantages will appear if you use computer-aided design (CAD) programs, such as AutoCAD or AutoSketch, or if your programs are concerned with elaborate calculations and are capable of using a co-processor.

If you find that your use of the XT type of computer (see Chapter 2 for the use of co-processors with the AT machines) would justify the fitting of the 8087 co-processor, how do you go about it?

- The first point is that your computer must be fitted with a socket to accept the 8087, and if this is not fitted you will have to look for an expansion board that will house the chip – you are not likely to find anything suitable.

- It is normal to have an empty socket (Figure 1.9) on the main circuit board of the XT or XT-clone into which the 8087 can be plugged. This can be done for you by a dealer if you do not feel inclined to use your computer like a Meccano set.

If you make the upgrade for yourself, the 8087 chip has to be selected with some care. The 8087 is a complicated chip, and selection at the factory results in several different grades of 8087 being available. Of these, the cheapest (about £70 in the UK if you shop around) will run at the 4 MHz clock speed of the original XT machine using the 8088 processor; a few clones also use this clock speed.

o These 8087 chips will not, however, run at the higher clock speeds that are used in some 8088 clones and almost universally for the 8086 machines, so that you have to select the 8087 to match the speed of your main microprocessor chip.

The usual versions of 8087 are for 5 MHZ, 8 MHz (suitable for Amstrads) and, less commonly, 10 MHz, and the faster chips command higher prices. At the time of writing, clone co-processors had just become available, resulting in all prices dropping considerably.

AT co-processors

The addition of the 8087 co-processor chip to an XT type of machine very considerably speeds the performance of a computer which is running any program that depends heavily on floating-point arithmetic.

o More advanced derivatives of the 8087 are available for the machines based on the 80286 and 80386 chips, but the advantages of using these more expensive co-processors are not quite so obvious and clear-cut even for users of large spreadsheets.

This is particularly true of the 80287, because the design of the 80286 is such that floating-point arithmetic can be carried out much more efficiently than on the older 8086 design in any case. Another problem is that the design of the 80286 and 80287 does not allow the two processors to work together in the way that the 8086 and 8087 can work simultaneously. The result of these factors is that the 80287 chip, despite its former £150 - £300 price tag (depending on clock speed) does not achieve such a dramatic increase in processing speed of spreadsheets, and for some software may actually reduce the processing speed.

● This bizarre effect arises because all arithmetic computation is handed to the 80287 if the chip is in its socket, and since the 80286 can handle integer arithmetic faster than the 80287, extensive use of integer arithmetic in a program can result in the 80287 processing this work more slowly than the 80286.

- Another problem is that the 80287 is always run at a slower clock speed than the 80286.

This, however, does not alter the fact that the addition of a co-processor on an 80286 or 80386 machine will substantially reduce the time needed when running programs such as CAD and spreadsheets which rely heavily on floating-point computations. The advantages are particularly noticeable when using CAD programs such as AutoCAD.

The 80387 remedies some of these problems, but it does not run along with the 80386 in the way that the 8087 runs along with the 8086 or 8088, and the same is true of the SX versions of the chips.

- Once again, the result is that though the 80387 chip, once priced at around £300 upwards, can speed up floating-point arithmetic on a 386 machine, the increase in speed is not so dramatic as on the 8088/8086 machines.

- Some users of 386 machines would notice no significant increase, certainly not proportionate to the cost, it they used only word processors and data-processing software.

This does not mean that the principle of the co-processor is no longer valid, because the co-processor is still the best way of tackling large number of floating-point calculations, and for the programs that make such calculations the gain in time is very useful.

A more recent development is co-processors from other manufacturers, notably iIT and Cyrix. These sell for much lower prices than the original Intel levels, and their immediate effect has been to cause a reduction in the prices of the Intel chips, making co-processors a much more attractive proposition to the user who needs it.

o The performance of these other chips is not necessarily identical to that of the Intel chips, and some care has to be taken over selection of a co-processor for any given application.

In some cases, there are (minor) errors in floating-point calculations which are not present when the Intel chips are used and though this probably matters very little for applications such as CAD, it can be important when floating-point calculations are used for specialist software, such as stress analysis.

Speeding compilers and databases

The speed performance of compilers and databases – programs such as Turbo Pascal and dBASE 4 – can be improved significantly by using the MS-DOS FASTOPEN utility. The improvements that this renders for other types of programs are not sufficient to warrant using it unless a compiler or database is the main software that is used.

FASTOPEN is a form of cache, but instead of caching data it maintains a memory record of the location of files on the hard disk. This allow files to be fetched and stored much more rapidly because the time needed to find the file location on the disk is eliminated.

o FASTOPEN can be used only for files on a hard disk, and cannot be used over a network.

FASTOPEN should be invoked from AUTOEXEC.BAT and never by selecting the command from any shell program such as DOSSHELL or Windows. The FASTOPEN program can make use of conventional memory or expanded (*not* extended memory).

o This is another justification for using EMM386.EXE to create some expanded memory on a 386 machine.

A typical line in the AUTOEXEC.BAT file would be:

```
FASTOPEN C:=80 D:=50
```

to allow 80 files to be held for drive C and 50 for drive D. The default number of files is 48. Adding /X will allow FASTOPEN to hold its file information in expanded memory.

- Using SMARTDrive, particularly the latest version for Windows 3.1, is much more effective for most applications. With SMARTDrive in use, adding FASTOPEN is not likely to show any advantages. If you have not enough memory to use SMARTDrive effectively, FASTOPEN may be more useful to you.

- Do not try to use FASTOPEN and SMARTDrive together.

Memory driver conflicts

Conflicts of memory managers are rare if you are using a single (non-networked) computer. If a conflict arises it will almost certainly be due to one of a few causes:

1 The use of two or more memory managers from different sources

2 The use of memory-resident software that conflicts with memory managers

3 The incorrect order of commands in the CONFIG.SYS file or (less likely) the AUTOEXEC.BAT file

Each of these is comparatively simple to sort out, though the job can be time-consuming. Remember in particular that a change to the CONFIG.SYS file takes no effect until the machine is rebooted. If you change the AUTOEXEC.BAT file you can type AUTOEXEC as a command to force the file to run.

- Check the memory managers that you use. Unless you have an expanded memory board that needs an EEMS driver of its own, you seldom need to use software other than HIMEM.SYS and EMM386.EXE.

- The Setup program for MS-DOS 5.0 will not install HIMEM.SYS if another extended-memory manager is working, but this does not prevent you from adding HIMEM.SYS for yourself at some later time, causing conflict.

- If your memory managers are blameless, try booting with a CONFIG.SYS file that contains only the bare essentials of memory-resident programs. You can then add programs one by one until the conflict re-appears (or, if you suspect one particular program, remove it from the main AUTOEXEC.BAT file).

- Remember that most machines will boot from a floppy in preference to the hard disk if there is a floppy in the A: drive.

- If the conflict persists with a fairly simple CONFIG.SYS file, check the order of commands; for example, HIMEM.SYS must be used before EMM386.EXE.

Network problems

The vast majority of memory problems arise when another form of memory manager is used: the *network manager*. The network managing software must manage not just one machine but a set of machines, so that the possibilities for conflict become much greater.

- This book is not concerned primarily with networks, and the complications of networks are such that they can be dealt with in detail only by a book dealing with the type of network you are using.

One potent source of trouble with networks arises when you change to MS-DOS 5.0 and find that the network also needs to be upgraded to a more recent version. The known problems for major networks are noted in the MS-DOS 5.0 *Getting Started* booklet.

○ Remember that if you use a network which is not one of the 'big name' types you will need to dig out information from the suppliers. Some suppliers, such as EQ Consultants (for the $25 Network) are notably helpful and informative; others are not (and their network software is often seen offered at large discounts).

The following is a selection of problems to illustrate the type of causes of conflict that can arise.

1 LAN Manager V.2 Enhanced has a NET START command which loads a file called NETWKSTA.EXE into the UMB region. This requires EMM386.EXE to have been used ahead of this command, and if LOADHIGH is used for NET START there will be problems, since it loads high anyway. A similar situation affects the REDIR.EXE command of LAN Manager Basic V2 and all files of LAN Manager V1. If you have any remaining space in the upper memory area you can load LAN Manager services such as NETPOPUP in this area.

   If you get a NET3055 message you will need to change the LANMAN.INI file in one of two possible ways:

   If you used `EMM386 /ram`, put `LIM=YES` in the [workstation] section of the LANMAN.INI file.

   If you used `EMM386 /noems`, put `LIM=NO` in the [workstation] section of the LANMAN.INI file.

2 Novell NetWare should present no problems unless the Internetwork Packet Exchange files such as NVER, SYSCON or RCONSOLE are used along with DOSSHELL task swapping. To remedy this you need to extract some files from the MS-DOS 5 distribution disks. These files are called IPX.OB_ and TBMI2.CO_, and are in compressed form.

(1) To decompress the files you need to use the utility EXPAND.EXE in the form:

```
EXPAND A:\IPX.OB_ A:\TBMI2.CO_ C:\MSDOS
```

which, in this example, will place the expanded files IPX.OBJ and TBMI2.COM onto the hard disk MSDOS directory.

(2) Use the IPX.OBJ file to create a new IPX.COM file, following the methods shown in the Novell manuals.

(3) Start up the network using the new IPX.COM and NET5.COM files, then start TBMI2.COM.

(4) Start the program that previously caused problems with the Task Swapper of DOS-SHELL. Run the program and then exit.

(5) Display information on what has happened by typing:

```
tbmi2 /d
```

(6) If the value of Far Call Usage is not 0, then you will always need to run TBMI2.COM before using Task Swapper.

To get help with TBMI2.COM, type TBMI2 /?.

The defaults for TBMI2.COM are suitable for most programs, and Novell will advise if you need to use any options for configuration.

Note that TBMI2.COM should not be run if you use Windows 3.0; see later for its use with Windows 3.1.

3 Artisoft LANtastic 3 may need the expanded memory area provided by EMM386.EXE to be altered, using:

```
EMM386 /X:D800 DFFF
```

to exclude the region used by the LAN manager.

4 Sitka TOPS should not use LOADHIGH for any of its TOPS files.

Windows and networks

If networking is a potent source of memory conflicts, using Windows along with networking is a
certain recipe for headaches, because the memory
managers of networks are almost certain to conflict
with the memory use by Windows.

o The most important advice in this respect is that
  if you encounter no problems running Windows
  over your network you have been lucky (or very
  skilful) and you should alter nothing that might
  upset this happy chance.

The most common problem is slow loading and
running, something that practically all networked
Windows users complain of. If Windows can be
used locally, on the local hard disk, the usual
remedies of SMARTDrive and using a permanent
swap file (see Chapters 4, 5) will greatly speed up
Windows use.

● The use of local Windows may be undesirable,
  however, and you may need to face the problems
  of speeding up Windows when only one copy is
  being run in the network server machine.

● This is made difficult because SMARTDrive cannot work over a network drive and you cannot
  create a permanent swap file on a network drive
  either.

1 If there is a local hard disk on each networked
  machine, using this for a permanent swap file,
  SMARTDrive, and keep on it the files that are
  used only by that workstation (which are not
  shared by other users).

2 For a workstation with adequate memory, set up
  a RAMdrive for temporary files.

3 Run Windows in standard mode, which is always
  faster.

The second common problem is to find that Windows will not run because of insufficient memory.

The remedy, almost every time, is to ensure that as much of the network software as possible is loaded into UMB space to release conventional memory.

o This may be done by default by some network managers, so that you do not need to specify a LOADHIGH command.

The amount of disk space used on each workstation need not be large, because most of the Windows files are in the main server. At most, each workstation should need only 160 Kb of the files that are installed in each local station by the SETUP command when a network is specified.

o This can be reduced, because a lot of the files simply duplicate the work of others that will already exist on the local disk. Similarly, there is no need to have on the server files that already exist in each workstation.

The next most common problem is that trying to use Windows causes a hang-up or brings everything back to the MS-DOS prompt (such as C>). This is the classic indication of a conflict of some sort.

● A total hang-up that requires the use of the reset button is almost always due to memory conflict, and the memory conflict is almost always in the UMB area, because of the use of UMB for buffers by both Windows and the network software.

● One remarkably simple solution is to run Windows in standard mode. Not only does this avoid the use of buffers in UMB, it also makes Windows run faster.

If you need to be able to use Windows at each workstation in 386 enhanced mode, the remedy involves some detective work with memory analysing software.

1 Find out how UMB memory is used by the network.

2 Exclude these sections of memory from use by Windows, or include some section outside these areas. Both methods require you to edit the Windows SYSTEM.INI file.

- To exclude an area of memory, use EMMEXCLUDE= *mmmm nnnn* in the [386Enh] portion of the SYSTEM.INI file. The letters *mmmm* and *nnnn* represent the hexadecimal address numbers for the part of memory to be excluded. Using EMMEXCLUDE=A000 FFFF will exclude all of the Upper Memory and make windows place its buffers into conventional memory.

- To make Windows use a definite piece of memory, use an EMMINCLUDE=*mmmm nnnn* line, also in the [386Enh] part of the SYSTEM.INI file. The hexadecimal addresses in this case should indicate the largest piece of UMB that is available and not used by the network.

When Windows starts and then fails, returning the screen to the MS-DOS prompt, the usual cause is an interrupt conflict rather than a memory conflict.

○ An interrupt is a signal to the microprocessor which forces the chip to stop what it is doing and attend to some other task. The nature of the task is fixed by using a number code for each interrupt.

The culprit responsible for most Windows interrupt problems is IRQ 2, and there can also be trouble from IRQ numbers 9 through to 16. The supplier of the network has to be approached for a solution to this, and Novell have a set of files that will attend to such problems with all Netware networks.

This brief set of examples takes in the most common problems, and shows a few of the known answers, but in many cases the solutions have to be individually worked out because no two networks are identical, and no two machines have their memory identically utilised.

Windows 3.1 includes updated versions of several Novell NetWare files with improvements and bug fixes that make it easier to use Netware with Windows 3.1. When you notify to Windows Setup that you are using Novell NetWare, the following files will be copied to your Windows directory:

```
NETX.COM
IPX.OBJ
IPXODI.COM
LSL.COM
TBMI2.COM
```

Before running Windows 3.1 you need to replace and upgrade some other files.

1 Replace your current NetWare shell with the NETX.COM program that is provided with Windows 3.1.

   The current shell may be called by any of the names:

```
NET3.COM      XMSNET3.COM      EMSNET3.COM
NET4.COM      XMSNET4.COM      EMSNET4.COM
NET5.COM      XMSNET5.COM      EMSNET5.COM
NETX.COM      XMSNETX.COM      EMSNETX.COM
```

   The new NETX.COM will run on any version of MS-DOS, and the EMS or XMS versions NETX can be obtained from Microsoft if required.

2 If you use Novell's IPXODI.COM and LSL.COM, you should upgrade these to the versions provided with Windows 3.1.

3 If you intend to run Windows 3.1 in standard mode for speed, you should load the TBMI2.COM memory-resident utility when running Windows rather than before starting Windows.

Appendices

Appendix A: Hexadecimal codes

All computing depends on the use of number codes. Some of the numbers are used to refer to locations in memory, each of which is numbered, some are used to mean commands, characters (using ASCII code) and other references. Each of these numbers is internally a set of 1s and 0s, as outlined in Chapter 1.

Binary code like this is fine for machines, because with only two possibilities to work with, the chances of the machine making a mistake become very remote. Humans, however, are not ideally suited to working in binary numbers without making mistakes, simply because the stream of 1s and 0s becomes confusing, and an obvious step is to use a more convenient number scale.

Just what is a more convenient number scale is quite another matter. Most people work with the ordinary 0-9 scale of denary numbers, based on counting in tens. Memory-analysing programs like Manifest, and memory management programs of all types, however, are written as much for the convenience of professional programmers, who use hexadecimal numbers, as for the ordinary computer user.

Hexadecimal means scale of sixteen, and the reason that it is used so extensively is that it is naturally suited to representing binary bytes. Four bits, half of a byte, will represent numbers which lie in the range 0 to 15 in our ordinary number scale.

o This is the range of one hex digit (see table on next page). Since we don't have symbols for digits higher than 9, we have to use the letters A, B, C, D, E and F to supplement the digits 0 to 9 in the hex scale.

The advantage is that a byte of data can be represented by a two-digit number, and a complete address by a five-digit number. Converting between binary and hex is much simpler than converting be-

Denary	Hex	Binary
0	00	0000
1	01	0001
2	02	0010
3	03	0011
4	04	0100
5	05	0101
6	06	0110
7	07	0111
8	08	1000
9	09	1001
10	0A	1010
11	0B	1011
12	0C	1100
13	0D	1101
14	0E	1110
15	0F	1111
16	10	10000

tween binary and denary. The number that we write as 10 (ten) in denary is written as 0A in hex, eleven as 0B, twelve as 0C and so on up to fifteen, which is 0F. The zero doesn't have to be written, but programmers get into the habit of writing a data byte with two digits and an address with four or more even if fewer digits are needed.

○ The number that follows 0F is 10, sixteen in denary, and the scale then repeats to 1F, thirty-one, which is followed by 20. The maximum size of byte, 255 in denary, is FF in hex.

When we write hex numbers, it's usual to mark them in some way so that we don't confuse them with denary numbers. There's not much chance of confusing a number like 3E with a denary number, but a number like 26 might be hex or denary. The convention that is followed by many programmers is to use a capital H to mark a hex number, with the H-sign placed after the number. Most of the

MS-DOS and DR-DOS memory utilities assume that you will type in hex numbers, and they will not work with anything else, and addresses in Manifest make use of hex numbers also.

Before we can get much further with addresses and their contents, we need to look at the way that addresses are organised. Because the 8088 and 8086 chips were developed from the older 8-bit 8088 type, there has been a strong family resemblance, and one thing that has carried over is the storing of numbers in 16-bit units: one-word units.

Now one word of 16 bits can represent scale-of-ten numbers from 0 to 65536, which is hex 0000H to FFFFH, a range of 64 Kb, but the construction of the 8088, 8086 and 80286 chips allows for the use of 20-bit numbers for addresses. This makes the hex range of numbers 00000 to FFFFF, 0 to 1048575. The ordinary 0 - 640 Kb range of memory uses the numbers 00000 to 9FFFF, and the rest of the memory uses the numbers A0000 to FFFFF. These numbers are split into two four-digit groups: the segment number and the displacement number.

All of the Intel processors from 8088 to 80286 make use of these two address numbers in the same way. An address is created by adding the numbers, but not in a straightforward way. The numbers are placed with the segment number shifted one place to the left, so that adding A000 to 0100 will give A0100, a five-digit number. For the 80386 and 80486 processors, the address can consist of a full 32-bit set such as 17FE2A55 in hex. This can be converted to the 5-digit form when the chip is being used with MS-DOS. The higher numbers could be used for virtual memory under a suitable operating system.

The numbers that are shown for memory addresses by MEM and other programs are the segment numbers, the first four hex digits of each memory number. An address of A000 therefore refers to the 64 Kb of memory from A0000 to AFFFF.

Appendix B: Suppliers of RAM and other memory-related products

Hardware

Chipboards,
Almac House,
Church Lane,
Bisley,
Woking,
Surrey GU24 9DR

Tel: (0483) 797959
Fax: (0493) 797702

Suppliers of complete systems and a huge variety of components and add-on boards.

RSC Corporate Computing,
75 77 Queens Road,
Watford,
Herts WD1 2QN

Tel: (0923) 243301
Fax: (0923) 237946

Suppliers of complete systems and a very comprehensive range of components.

DABS Press,
22 Warwick St.,
Prestwich,
Manchester M25 6LZ

Tel: (061) 773 8632
Fax: (061) 773 8290

Supply assembled systems, a large range of components, software and books.

Matmos Ltd.,
Unit 11,
Lewes Road,
Lindfield,
W. Sussex RH16 2LX

Tel: (0444) 482091 / 483830
Fax: (0444) 484258

An old-established supplier of computer components, and also complete systems at low prices.

Microsurgeons (Isenstein) Ltd.,
Deeside Industrial Estate,
Welsh Road,
Deeside,
Clwyd CH5 2LR

Tel: (0244) 281025
Fax: (0244) 281161

Supply a large range of low-cost computers with excellent specifications, and a full range of memory chips and SIMMs for their own machines (usable also by most other compatible machines).

Cricklewood Electronics Ltd.,
40 Cricklewood Broadway,
London NW2 3ET

Tel: (081) 452 0161 or (081) 450 0995
Fax: (0810 208 1441
Telex: 914977 CRIKEL G

Supply chips of all types, sockets, tools, cables and all forms of electronic components, kits and assemblies.

Maplin Electronics,
P.O. Box 3,
Rayleigh,
Essex SS6 8LR

One of the largest mail-order supplier of electronic components of all types, and also an excellent range of books.

Software

Public Domain Software Library
The PDSL exists to supply disks of programs that are virtually free for inspection, and the only cost to the user is the cost of copying the disks. PDSL can supply on a range of disk formats, and in some cases are virtually the only source of software for some exotic machines. All of the programs are either public domain or shareware. Documentation for each program is included as a disk file, usually with the DOC extension.

A public domain program is one for which the author has surrendered all copyright, allowing the program to be copied freely by anyone who wants to use it (the way schools used to copy textbooks when photocopying came out of an unlimited budget and books came out of a carefully rationed budget). Many public domain programs are short utilities, and you would normally buy them on a disk that contained 20 - 50 such items. Other PD programs are distinctly longer, and though some of them do not have the polish of a commercial program they must have represented hundreds of hours of effort. The writers are often professional programmers working at a hobby topic and glad to share the results of their efforts.

Shareware is a rather different concept. The author of a shareware package is hoping to sell directly to the user, cutting out the overheads that are involved in having a program manufactured and distributed commercially. In the early days of shareware, the programs were full working versions, and the poor response by way of payment was a severe blow to authors, particularly in the UK, where users were always less willing to pay for programs than in the USA where the idea started. It has become more common now for shareware programs to be limited to some extent, perhaps running on only a single video card, or unable to use a printer or to create disk files. The user can run the program to a sufficient extent to see if it is likely to be useful, and will have lost very little if it is not. Registering with the author can be done directly (it is easy to phone an author in the USA and quote a credit card number) or by way of the PDSL if this can be arranged.

Registration can often be done at various levels, with the minimum level entitling you to a copy of the program with all limitations removed. The documentation will be, as for PD items, as a DOC or READ.ME file on the disk. At a higher fee, a full manual is provided and the user is entitled to upgrades at nominal cost.

The address for PDSL is:

Winscombe House,
Beacon Road,
Crowborough,
E. Sussex TN6 1UL

Tel: (0892) 663298
Fax: (0892) 667473

At the time of writing, membership subscriptions were £21 per annum for private membership, £69 per annum for corporate membership, and disks were copied for prices of £3.75 each (members) or £5.00 (non-members) with discounts for quantities. There is a surcharge, currently 90p, for 3½" 720K disks.

Quarterdeck Office Systems (UK) Ltd.,
Widford Hall,
Widford Hall Lane,
Chelmsford,
Essex CM2 8TD

Tel: (0245) 496699
Fax: (0245) 495284

This is the main UK office of Quarterdeck, which offers technical support for all of their products as well as acting as a sales and information centre. Separate voice and fax numbers are available for registered users who need technical help. The latest memory manager at the time of writing is QEMM-386 V6, which allows extended memory to be managed flexibly so that the correct format of memory is available to whatever program requires it; this allowsw a program that needs expanded memory to be used along with one that requires extended memory without the need to reboot with a different CONFIG.SYS file. QEMM 386 V6 also allows the addresses used by ROM on most machines to be used for RAM by switching from ROM to RAM or back as required.

> EQ Consultants,
> New Gilston,
> Leven,
> Fife KY8 5TF
>
> Tel: (0334) 84248
> Fax: (0334) 84482

Suppliers of the $25 Network for up to three machines, using serial ports at high speed. This simple network allows you to control remote drives and printers, with a memory overhead of only 15 Kb. Full telephone support is provided, and cables can also be supplied if needed.

> Ctrl-Alt-Deli (CAD),
> 26 North 12th St.,
> Central Milton Keynes,
> MK9 3BT
>
> Tel: (0908) 662759
> Fax: (0908) 606104

A source of software that is not usually available from any other UK supplier, including the remarkable More Windows utility. Main distributors of the PC Tools package, and also of various useful screen-grab and other utilities.

Appendix C: Books

The following books are available on memory and hard disk use, use of memory management programs, shells and utilities.

Hard Disks Step by Step
by Ian Sinclair (Butterworth Heinemann)

Using Disk and RAM Utilities Step by Step
by Ian Sinclair (Butterworth Heinemann)

Mastering DESQView
by Ian Sinclair (Sigma Press)

MS-DOS 5.0 File & Program Control
by Ian Sinclair (Sigma Press)

Newnes Windows 3 Pocket Book
by Ian Sinclair (Butterworth Heinemann)

Appendix D: Advice on specific programs

The following programs are a small selection of popular software that are know to be able to use memory outside the 640 Kb barrier. The list excludes all Windows products, because for such programs, Windows itself carries out memory management. In addition, the networking use of these programs is also excluded because some programs can be used over networks without modification, others require the purchase of special networking versions, and the problems that are encountered depend on the network used as well as on the program. Except where stated, the programs in this list use expanded memory, so that their use of extra memory is dependent on either an expanded memory board being fitted (8088, 8086, 80286) or the EMM386.EXE memory manager being used to convert some extended memory to expanded in 80386 and 80486 machines. The methods shown here are typical of those used on other programs that are not listed.

WordPerfect and LetterPerfect

WordPerfect and LetterPerfect can make use of expanded memory to any LIM specification higher than 3.2. When no expanded memory is available, the data will be stored on the hard disk, so that the use of expanded memory is a useful way of speeding up the action of these word processors.

o The use of extended memory is not directly supported (WordPerfect for Windows has access to all Windows use of extended memory).

If WordPerfect or LetterPerfect are used along with other programs in a multi-tasking way, and if expanded memory is available, the amount of conventional memory used by the Perfect programs can be restricted by using the /W option when starting the program. The /W option needs to be followed by two figures separated by a comma:

1 The first figure is the amount of conventional memory to be used. The asterisk can be placed here to mean all of the conventional memory (the default).

2 The second figure is the amount of expanded memory to be used, and the asterisk will mean all of it. If the second figure and the comma are omitted, all of the expanded memory will be used.

For example, starting LetterPerfect with:

```
LP /W=120/1024
```

will allow LetterPerfect to use only 120 Kb of conventional memory and 1024 Kb of expanded. Using `LP /W=120` would restrict LetterPerfect to 120 Kb of conventional memory and as much expanded memory as could be found.

o Using the /32 option allows the use of LIM 3.2 commands, and can sometimes help with using memory boards (on old XT machines) that are not LIM 4.0 compatible.

Using the /R option allows parts of the main programs to be loaded into expanded memory, with a considerable gain in speed.

Overflow files, used to keep parts of a document that cannot be fitted into conventional memory, are usually kept on hard disk, using the same directory as houses the main files of the program. By using the /D option you can place these files on a RAM disk for faster operation. The letter D is followed by a dash and the drive letter in the form:

```
/D E:\
```

This example specifies a drive lettered as E.

o You can use a /NE option if you do not want to make use of expanded memory at all.

De Luxe Paint-II
De Luxe Paint-II is the enduring painting package for the PC and some other machines. It requires a full 640 Kb of conventional memory, preferably free of TSR programs, so that as many TSRs as possible

should be loaded into UMB space. De Luxe Paint-II will make use of expanded memory if it detects an expanded memory manager program.

Expanded memory is particularly desirable if you need to use the commands Fix Background (see below), Stencil, Brush Flip, Brush Rotate and Brush Double.

o The use of expanded memory is essential if De Luxe Paint-II is used along with an E-VGA graphics card.

Expanded memory *must* be present if you want to use the Fix Background ability of De Luxe Paint-II, which allows you to place a drawing in the background and paint on top of it, as if on a glass sheet, without altering the background.

o If a RAMdisk is in use, it can be specified for swapping the spare page that De Luxe Paint-II can create and work with.

AutoCAD and AutoSketch

AutoCAD and AutoSketch both require expanded memory if large drawings are to be used. A co-processor is also desirable. The following comments refer mainly to AutoSketch because AutoCAD is a program of much greater complexity which is from the same suppliers.

The Memory Meter display of AutoSketch shows use of memory, and if any drawing approaches 100% use it needs to be saved until such time as more memory can be provided. AutoSketch can use up to 2 Mb of expanded memory for drawings.

In addition, a RAMdisk can be used for the temporary files that AutoSketch produces. This requires you to make use of the two environment variables ASUNDO and ASVECT, placed in lines in the AUTOEXEC.BAT file or whatever batch file is used to start AutoSketch. For example, if the RAMdisk is E, the lines:

```
SET ASUNDO=E:\
SET ASVECT=E:\
```

will attend to placing temporary files on the RAMdisk.

AutoSketch normally uses all of the expanded memory it can find, but an environment variable can be used to prevent expanded memory from being used if its use by AutoSketch might cause conflicts. The line:

```
SET ASLIMEM=OFF
```

in the batch file will prevent expanded memory from being used.

The ASMEMPATH environment variable is used to indicate a path for storing drawing and associated temporary files when there is not enough space in conventional memory. The action of AutoSketch is greatly speeded up if this path points to a RAMdisk, but only if the RAMdisk is of sufficient size. A size of 1 Mb may be necessary.

For example, using in the AUTOEXEC.BAT of other batch file the line:

```
SET ASMEMPATH=E:\
```

would ensure the use of a RAMdrive E: for these files. The RAMdrive size should be at least twice the size of the largest drawing file you are likely to use 512 Kb is usually safe for AutoSketch use.

o The use of these environmental variables is an *alternative* to the use of expanded memory, not an accompaniment. If you have enough expanded memory it will be used automatically.

Aldus PageMaker
Aldus PageMaker is one of the leading high-price Windows DTP programs, and one which requires as much memory as can be obtained. PageMaker runs under Windows, so that it makes use of the extended memory under the control of windows, and the hints on using Windows (Chapter 4) apply when PageMaker is to be used. The conventional memory should be cleared as far as possible, relocating any indispensable TSRs to UMB space.

Page Plus
Page Plus is also a Windows-based DTP program to which the same remarks apply, though it is not

quite so demanding of conventional memory space as PageMaker.

Lotus 1-2-3 V2.2

This version of 1-2-3 is intended to be used with 8088, 8086 and small capacity 80286 machines. It can make use of up to 4 Mb of expanded memory to LIM specification, and will do so automatically if there is expanded memory present.

Lotus 1-2-3 (3.0 or Later)

These programs present special problems. If you run Lotus 1-2-3 V3.0 along with the Task Swapper in DOSSHELL, you will need to set the *XMS Memory KB Required* option (in the Advanced dialogue box) to 384.

If you are using Lotus 1-2-3 3.0 or later, and you load device drivers or memory-resident programs into the upper memory area, always use the RAM switch with the `DEVICE=EMM386.EXE` command in the CONFIG.SYS file.

o If you use /NOEMS you will find that Lotus 1-2-3 will not run because it needs to be able to use some expanded memory – this and any other program described as using a VCPI (Virtual Control Program Interface) make use of extended memory by way of a small piece of expanded memory which must be present and available.

Index

NEWNES POCKET BOOKS - COMPLETE LISTING

A series of handy, inexpensive, pocket sized reference books to be kept by the computer or at your place of work and used every day. Their size makes them ideal "travelling" companions as well.

All titles are hardback.

COMPUTING

Newnes Software Engineer's Pocket Book
Newnes C Pocket Book
Newnes C + + Pocket Book
Newnes Hard Disk Pocket Book
Newnes Mac Users Pocket Book
Newnes MS DOS Pocket Book
Newnes PC Printers Pocket Book
Newnes PC Users Pocket Book
Newnes UNIX Pocket Book
Newnes Windows 3/3.1 Pocket Book
Newnes Upgrading Your PC Pocket Book
Newnes Upgrading Your Macintosh Pocket Book

ENGINEERING

Newnes Data Communications Pocket Book

Newnes Computer Engineer's
Pocket Book
Newnes 68000 Family Pocket Book
Newnes Microprocessor Pocket Book
Newnes Z80 Pocket Book
Newnes 8086 Pocket Book
Newnes Electronics Pocket Book
Newnes Engineering Science
Pocket Book
Newnes Instrumentation &
Measurement Pocket Book
Newnes Audio and Hi-Fi Engineer's
Pocket Book
Newnes Electrical Engineer's
Pocket Book
Newnes Electronics Assembly
Pocket Book
Newnes Electronics Circuits
Pocket Book
Newnes Engineering Materials
Pocket Book
Newnes Mathematics Pocket Book
Newnes Mechanical Engineer's
Pocket Book
Newnes Physical Sciences
Pocket Book
Newnes Radio Amateurs Listeners
Pocket Book
Newnes Radio Electronics Engineer's
Pocket Book
Newnes Refrigeration Technician
Pocket Book
Newnes TV and Video Engineer's
Pocket Book

This series, designed for clarity and ease of use, is intended for those who wish to get off to a flying start when faced with new software, operating systems or machines. These books take you through, step-by-step, the processes and functions that will enable you to maximise your effectiveness FAST.

The books are written by users for users and are now published in association with PC PLUS, the UK's best-selling PC-specific magazine. The Step by Step series and PC PLUS magazine provide the complete package for all IBM - Compatible personal computer users.

WORDPROCESSORS

Using Locoscript PC (Version 1.5)
John Campbell
0 7506 0249 X £14.95

Using MS Word 5.0
Roger Carter
0 434 90316 7 £14.95

Using Word for Windows
Alan Balfe
0 7506 0205 8 £14.95

Using Wordperfect for Windows
Arthur Tennick
0 7506 0359 3 £14.95

Using Wordperfect 5.0
Gautier
0 434 90656 5 £14.95

Using Wordstar 5, 5.5 & 6
Alan Balfe
0 7506 0341 0 £14.95

SPREADSHEETS

Using Excel 3.0
Roger Carter
0 7506 0360 7 £14.95

Using Lotus 1-2-3 Macros
Ian Sinclair
0 7506 0198 1 £16.95

Lotus 1-2-3 for Windows
Arthur Tennick
0 7506 0607 X £14.95

Using Lotus 1-2-3 Release 3
Stephen Morris
0 434 91292 1   £14.95

Quattro Pro 3
P K McBride
0 7506 0358 5   £14.95

DATABASES

Paradox 3.5 for Windows
P K McBride
0 7506 0610 X   £14.95

Using Q & A
Roger Carter
0 4349 0224 1   £14.95

Using Superbase 2 & 4
Arthur Tennick
0 7506 0042 X   £14.95

Using dBASE IV
Roger Carter
0 434 90251 9   £14.95

UTILITIES

Using Disk & RAM Utilities
Ian Sinclair
0 434 91892 X   £14.95

OPERATING SYSTEMS

MS—Dos 5.0
Alan Balfe
0 7506 0471 9   £14.95

Windows 3/3.1
Arthur Tennick
0 7506 0740 8 £14.95

CP/M Plus on the Amstrad PCW
John Cambell
0 7506 0460 3 £14.95

Windows NT
Arthur Tennick
0 7506 0852 8 £14.95

MACHINE GUIDES

Exploiting the Amstrad PCW 9512
John Campbell & Marion Pye
0 7506 0075 6 £14.95

Using the Amstrad PC1512/1640
Second edition
Morris
0 434 91266 2 £14.95

PC Memory
Ian Sinclair
0 7506 0686 X £14.95

Using the Amstrad PCW9512
John Campbell
0 7506 0169 8 £12.95

Hard Disks
Ian Sinclair
0 7506 0684 3 £14.95

DESKTOP PUBLISHING

Ventura 3.0/4.0 for Windows
John Campbell
0 7506 0632 0   £14.95

Pagemaker 4.0 for Windows
Alan Balfe
0 7506 0634 7   £14.95

Corel Draw 2.0/2.01
John Cambell & Marion Pye
0 7506 0503 0   £14.95

Quark Xpress for Windows
Keith Brindley
0 7506 0851 X   £14.95

PROGRAMMING

Using Quick Basic 4.5
Stephen Morris
0 7506 0220 1   £14.95

Visual Basic
Stephen Morris
0 7506 0633 9   £14.95

Programming in G-W Basic
P K McBride
0 7506 0256 2   £14.95